EXPLAINING BIBLICAL INERRANCY

THE CHICAGO STATEMENTS ON BIBLICAL INERRANCY, HERMENEUTICS, AND APPLICATION WITH OFFICIAL ICBI COMMENTARY

THE INTERNATIONAL COUNCIL ON BIBLICAL INERRANCY

R.C. SPROUL

and

NORMAN L GEISLER

◥BASTION BOOKS◤

Explaining Biblical Inerrancy:

The Chicago Statements on Biblical Inerrancy, Hermeneutics, and Application with Official ICBI Commentary

By International Council on Biblical Inerrancy, R.C. Sproul, and Norman L. Geisler

Edited by Norman L. Geisler and Christopher T. Haun

Cover design by Kristen Chadbourne

Desktop publishing by Paul A. Compton

Copyright © 2013 Bastion Books. All rights reserved.

Published by

> Bastion Books
> P.O. Box 14644
> Arlington, TX 76094
> http://BastionBooks.com

The Chicago Statements on Biblical Inerrancy, Biblical Hermeneutics, and Biblical Application were reproduced with optical character recognition from scans of the original documents located at:

> https://library.dts.edu/Pages/TL/Special/ICBI-1978-11-07.pdf
> https://library.dts.edu/Pages/TL/Special/ICBI_2.pdf
> https://library.dts.edu/Pages/TL/Special/ICBI_3.pdf

Copyright © 1978, 1980, 1983 International Council on Biblical Inerrancy. All rights reserved.

Explaining Inerrancy: A Commentary is reproduced here with the permission of both Ligonier Ministries and R.C. Sproul. Copyright © 1996 Ligonier Ministries. All rights reserved.

Explaining Hermeneutics is reproduced here with the permission of Norman L. Geisler. Copyright © 1983 Norman L. Geisler. All rights reserved.

Photographs were copied with permission from the ICBI Archives at Dallas Theological Seminary.

CONTENTS

Foreword v

BOOK I
CSBI
The Chicago Statement on Biblical Inerrancy

Introduction	3
A Short Statement	5
Exposition	12

BOOK II
CSBH
The Chicago Statement on Biblical Hermeneutics

Introduction	23
Articles of Affirmation and Denial	25
Exposition	33

BOOK III
CSBA
The Chicago Statement on Biblical Application

Introduction	49
Preface	58
Articles of Affirmations and Denial	59

BOOK IV
EXPLAINING INERRANCY
A Commentary on the Chicago Statement

Foreword	79
COMMENTARY R.C. Sproul	83

BOOK V
EXPLAINING HERMENEUTICS
A Commentary on the Chicago Statement on Biblical Hermeneutics

COMMENTARY Norman L. Geisler	127

FOREWORD

It is a fact of human experience that when the living eye-witnesses to events die off, the process of developing myths about these events is often accelerated.[1] So, as one of the three living framers of the Chicago statements on inerrancy and hermeneutics, it seemed good to put the first two statements and their official commentaries in one inexpensive and universally accessible source.

Four Fundamental ICBI Documents

There were four ICBI documents on the meaning of inerrancy:

1. The Chicago Statement on Biblical Inerrancy (by the ICBI drafting committee, 1978)
2. The Commentary on the Chicago Statement on Biblical Inerrancy (by Dr. R. C. Sproul in 1980)
3. The Chicago Statement on Biblical Hermeneutics (by the ICBI drafting committee, 1982)
4. The Commentary on the Chicago Statement on Biblical Hermeneutics (by me in 1983)

These four documents, comprise the core of this book.

Dr. R. C. Sproul was not just a signer of the three ICBI statements. He was also the original framer of the affirmations and denials of the Chicago Statement on Biblical Inerrancy, the president of the ICBI during its tenure, and the author of the official commentary on the Chicago Statement on Biblical Inerrancy. His commentary was originally published as a booklet entitled *Explaining Inerrancy: A Commentary* (International Council on Biblical Inerrancy: 1980). It has been reproduced here with the permission of Dr. Sproul and Ligonier Ministries.

I was also a member of the ICBI drafting committee, the general editor and director of all the publications of the ICBI, and the author of the official commentary explaining the second Chicago Statement. My commentary was originally published as a booklet titled *Explaining Hermeneutics: A Commentary on the Chicago Statement on Biblical Hermeneutics* (International Council on Biblical Inerrancy: 1983).

Other Important ICBI Books

In addition, official ICBI books were produced on these two Statements. On the first Statement (1978), the book titled *Inerrancy*, ed. Norman L. Geisler (Zondervan, 1979) was produced, consisting of chapters by ICBI conference scholars. Also, there was *Hermeneutics, Inerrancy, and the Bible* (Zondervan, 1984) edited by Earl Radmacher and Robert Preus, consisting of papers from the ICBI hermeneutics summit in 1982. Gordon Lewis and Bruce Demarest put together, *Challenges to Inerrancy: A Theological Response* (Moody Press, 1984). Another ICBI book on the meaning of inerrancy was produced titled *Biblical Errancy: An Analysis of Its Philosophical Roots,* ed. Norman L. Geisler (Zondervan, 1981). The final book of the ICBI series was on the application of inerrant Bible in the Chicago Statement on Biblical Application (CSBA). It was edited by Kenneth S. Kantzer and titled *Applying the Scriptures: Papers from ICBI Summit III* (Zondervan, 1987).

Why the ICBI View on Inerrancy is So Important

As evangelicals we recognize that no extra-biblical statements or creeds are infallible. Only the Bible is infallible. Nonetheless, some doctrinal statements are very important. The ICBI statements fall into this category for many reasons. First, they stand in continuity with the historic orthodox view on Scripture (see John Hannah, *Inerrancy and the Church,* Moody, 1984). Second, it was put together by an international group of some 300 evangelical scholars, not by an individual or mere handful of persons. Third, it has been adopted (in 2003) as a guide in understanding inerrancy by the largest group of evangelical scholars in the world, the Evangelical Theological Society. Fourth, its views were adopted by the Southern Baptist Convention, one of the largest protestant denominations in the world, in a landmark turn-around which saved them from drifting into liberalism. Finally, it has become the standard view of evangelicalism in America on this topic, having been officially or unofficially widely adopted as the guideline on the meaning of the inspiration and inerrancy of the Bible in numerous schools, churches, and Christian organizations.

The Purposes of this Book

As general editor of the International Council on Biblical Inerrancy (ICBI) books, a member of the ICBI drafting committee, and the author of the ICBI official commentary on the ICBI hermeneutics statement, my purpose in this book is twofold. First, my desire is to make all four foundational ICBI documents available in one volume for this and future generations to study. Second, I hope this will help dispel some contemporary misinterpretations of what the ICBI framers meant by inerrancy. There are several issues to which we wish to draw attention.

Misunderstanding about the Meaning of the Concept of "Truth" in the ICBI Statement

One of the most important misunderstandings of the ICBI statements hinges upon what the framers meant by the biblical view of truth mentioned in Article XIII of *The Chicago Statement on Biblical Inerrancy* (1978). It reads: "We deny that it is proper to evaluate Scripture according to standards of truth and error that are alien to its usage or purpose." Some mistakenly took this to justify an intentionalist view of truth and inerrancy which states that the Bible is only true in what it *intends* to affirm, not necessary in all that it *actually* affirms. But this is contrary to what the ICBI framers meant by inerrancy, as is revealed in its official commentary on those very articles. ICBI declared explicitly "When we say that the truthfulness of Scripture ought to be evaluated according to its own standards that means that ... **all the claims of the Bible must correspond with reality**, whether that reality is historical, factual or spiritual."[2] It adds, "**By biblical standards of truth and error is meant the view used both in the Bible and in everyday life, viz., a correspondence view of truth.** This part of the article is directed toward those who would redefine truth to relate merely to redemptive intent, the purely personal, or the like, rather than to mean that which corresponds with reality."

Misunderstanding about the Function of Genre in Scripture

The second major misinterpretation of the ICBI statements centers on the use of genre in the interpretation of Scripture. Article XVIII of *The Chicago Statement on Biblical Inerrancy* (1978) reads: "We affirm that the text of Scripture is to be interpreted by grammatico-historical exegesis, **taking account of its literary forms and devices**, and that Scripture is to interpret Scripture" (emphasis added). Likewise, Article XIII asserts, "We affirm that awareness of the literary categories, formal and stylistic, of the various parts of Scripture is essential for proper exegesis, and hence **we value genre criticism** as one of the many disciplines of biblical study" (emphasis added). Article XV adds, "We affirm the necessity of interpreting the Bible according to its literal, or normal sense. ... Interpretation according to the literal sense **will take account of all figures of speech and literary forms found in the text**" (emphasis added).[3]

From these statements some evangelical scholars have claimed ICBI blessing on the view that one can determine the meaning of a biblical text by first making a list of the kinds of genre from external sources and then applying what they believe is the appropriate genre to the Scriptures. However, the view that genre determines meaning is not only contrary to what the ICBI framers meant, but it also suffers from a logical mistake. In order to discover the genre of a particular text, one must already have a developed a genre theory. But a genre theory comes from studying and comparing individual texts of the Bible by means of the "grammatico-historical" (or grammatical-historical) method of interpretation which the ICBI framers were committed to from the beginning (see Article XVIII) of the Chicago Statement on Inerrancy. If externally determined genre governs the meaning of the biblical text, then this scenario is impossible. The interpreter must know the genre before he knows the text. This becomes tantamount to imposing genre expectations upon the text. In hermeneutics, this is labeled *eisegesis* (reading meaning into the text), rather an *exegesis* (reading meaning out of the text)! So, this widely used method of genre determination is contrary to the ICBI understanding of inerrancy.

*Misunderstanding of the Historical Nature
of Biblical Narratives*

From the beginning, ICBI spelled out its commitment to the historicity of the biblical narratives. Article XVIII of The Chicago Statement on Biblical Inerrancy (1978) reads: "We deny the legitimacy of any treatment of the text or quest for sources lying behind it that leads to relativizing, **dehistoricising**, or counting its teaching, or rejecting its claim to authorship" (emphasis added). The ICBI position became even more explicit in its Chicago Statement of Biblical Hermeneutics (1982). Article XIII declares: "**We deny that generic categories which negate historicity may rightly be imposed on biblical narratives** which present themselves as factual." Article XIV goes on to say, "**We deny that any event, discourse or saying reported in Scripture was invented by the biblical writers** or by the traditions they incorporated" (emphasis added).

The Chicago Statement on Biblical Inerrancy is clear on this issue. "We affirm the propriety of using inerrancy as a theological term with reference **to the complete truthfulness of Scripture**" (Article XIII). "We affirm that inspiration, though not conferring omniscience, **guaranteed true and trustworthy utterance on all matters of which the Biblical authors were moved to speak and write**" (Article IX). "**We affirm that Scripture in its entirety is inerrant, being free from all falsehood, fraud, or deceit.** We deny that Biblical infallibility and inerrancy are limited to spiritual, religious, or redemptive themes, exclusive of assertions in **the fields of history and science**" (Article XII). "We affirm the propriety of using inerrancy as a theological term with reference to **the complete truthfulness of Scripture**" (Article XII).

The ICBI commentary adds, "Though the Bible is indeed *redemptive* history, it is also redemptive *history*, and this means that the acts of salvation wrought by God actually occurred in the space-time world" (Article XII). With regard to the historicity of the Bible, Article XIII in the commentary points out that we should not "take Adam to be a myth, whereas in Scripture he is presented as a real person." Likewise, it affirms that we should not "take Jonah to be an allegory when he is presented as a historical person and [is] so referred to by Christ." It adds, "We further deny that scientific hypotheses about earth history may properly be used to overturn the teaching of Scripture on creation and the flood" (Article XII of the "Chicago Statement"). In short, the ICBI framers believed that using genre to deny any part of the historicity of the biblical record was a denial of inerrancy.

*Misunderstanding about the Relationship
between Hermeneutics and Inerrancy*

Another misunderstanding is the claim that the ICBI view is that inerrancy and hermeneutic are to be totally separated. In short, they claim that inerrancy simply affirms that whatever the Bible affirms is true, but only hermeneutics can inform us as to what the Bible is actually affirming. That is to say, it is just a matter of interpretation of the text and not a question of inerrancy. It is wrongly thought by some that ICBI made no specific claims on what the biblical text means or on whether the biblical narrative is historical as long as they believe that the text is inerrant—whatever it may mean. However, this is clearly not the case for many reasons.

The Total Separation of Hermeneutics and Inerrancy is not Logically Necessary

The ICBI framers foresaw this issue and spoke to it clearly. In brief, the ICBI response is that hermeneutics and inerrancy are *formally distinct*, but when it comes to the inerrancy of the Bible, they are *actually inseparable*. For example, Siamese twins with two heads and only one heart are inseparable but not identical. Apart from death, our soul and body are inseparable, but they are not identical. Hence, the charge that inerrancy and hermeneutics are identical does not necessarily follow logically.

A bifurcation of hermeneutics from inerrancy is empty, vacuous, and meaningless. This innovative view of the ICBI statements on inerrancy amounts to saying that the Bible is not teaching that anything is actually true. However, the ICBI statements repeatedly affirm that everything the Bible affirms is completely true. The "Chicago Statement" makes **"reference to the complete truthfulness of Scripture"** (Article XIII). It insists that it is **"trustworthy utterance on all matters of which the Biblical authors were moved to speak and write"** (Article IX). But these would be senseless claims, if the

Bible was not really making any claims about reality. So, the claim to inerrancy entails a certain kind of understanding of what the Bible means, namely, a grammatical-historical understanding of the text. This, along with the correspondence view of truth (see above) negate the claim that inerrancy as such is merely a vacuous claim that amounts to saying, "If the Bible is claiming that anything is true, then it is actually true, but inerrancy is not really claiming anything is actually true. Only hermeneutics can fill in this void." On the contrary, both the correspondence view of truth and the grammatical-historical view of interpretation demand that the doctrine of inerrancy as embraced by ICBI is claiming that the belief in biblical inerrancy entails actual truths about reality.

The ICBI Chicago Statement on Inerrancy includes a statement on the literal historical-grammatical hermeneutics. As noted above, Article XVIII reads: "We affirm that the text of Scripture is to be interpreted by grammatico-historical exegesis..." There are very good reasons for including this statement on hermeneutics in an evangelical inerrancy statement. For one thing, there would be no doctrine of inerrancy were it not for the grammatical-historical hermeneutic by which we derive inerrancy from Scripture. For another, the term "evangelical" implies a certain doctrinal stand on essential doctrines, including the inspiration of Scripture, the virgin birth, the deity of Christ, His atoning death, and His bodily resurrection. These doctrines expressed in the early Creeds of Christendom are derived from Scripture by the grammatical-historical hermeneutic. Without it there would be no "evangelical" or "orthodox" creeds or orthodox beliefs in accord with them. Thus, the ICBI evangelical view of inerrancy is wedded with a literal method of interpretation that affirms truth about the real world.

ICBI Claim to Inerrancy Involved a Claim to Objective Truth about Reality

Since ICBI embraced a correspondence view of truth which affirms that truth corresponds with reality, then when we say the Bible is completely true the statement cannot be empty. It must refer to some reality beyond itself. This is why ICBI included a statement about the literal grammatical-historical interpretation of the Bible as part of its articles about the meaning of inerrancy. Article XVIII says: "We affirm that the text of Scripture is to be interpreted by grammatical-historical exegesis. ..." In short, there is an overlap between inerrancy and hermeneutics because inerrancy is not an empty claim. It is a claim that involves the assertion that an inerrant Bible is actually true in all that it affirms. And this truth corresponds literally to the reality about which it speaks.

This is not to say that Bible does not use figures of speech, for Article XVIII clearly allows "taking account of literary forms and devices." It means that there is some literal referent for these figures of speech. Thus, inerrancy is not claiming that "If the Bible is making a truth claim, then that truth claim must be true." Rather, inerrancy claims that that "The Bible is making truth claims, and they are all true." Since truth is what corresponds to reality, to say the Bible is inerrant is to say that all of its claims correspond to reality. In this way there is a marriage, not a divorce, between inerrancy and the literal method of interpreting the Bible.

This disjunction between hermeneutics and inerrancy is an example of "methodological unorthodoxy."[4] If it were true, then one could completely allegorize the Bible—denying the literal Virgin Birth, physical resurrection of Christ, and everything else—and still claim that they held to the inerrancy of the Bible. This would mean that someone like Mary Baker Eddy, the founder of the Christian Science cult, could, even with a totally allegorical method, affirm that the ICBI statements on inerrancy are true, even though she does not believe in any evangelical doctrine, including the Inspiration of Scripture. It would also mean that someone could use a so-called Averronian method of "double truth" and still hold to an ICBI view of inerrancy. But it makes no sense to claim that the Bible is completely true in all that it affirms and yet deny that it affirms certain specific doctrines. In addition to unorthodox doctrines, there are also unorthodox methods. The grammatical-historical hermeneutics is an orthodox method accepted by ICBI. And an allegorical method is an unorthodox method. Likewise, New Testament scholars who deny the historicity of sections of the Gospel narratives are acting contrary to the meaning of the ICBI framers.

The Separation is Explicitly Contrary in Spirit and in Letter to the ICBI

The preface to the Chicago Statement on Biblical Hermeneutics made it clear that the ICBI framers saw hermeneutics as being inseparably connected to inerrancy. It says:

> The work of Summit I had hardly been completed when it became evident that there was yet another major task to be tackled. While we recognize that belief in the inerrancy of Scripture is basic to maintaining its authority, **the values of that commitment are only as real as one's understanding of the meaning of Scripture.** Thus, the need for Summit II. For two years plans were laid and papers were written on themes relating to hermeneutical principles and practices.

The very fact that there was a second ICBI summit is a clear indication of how the ICBI framers and signers judged this matter. The second ICBI summit is an expansion and elaboration of ARTICLE XVIII from the statement produced by the first ICBI Summit.

Concluding Comments

It is hoped that providing the primary sources for the ICBI view on inerrancy will help clarify these and other issues at stake in the current inerrancy debates. While every scholar is free to mean by inerrancy whatever he or she desires it to mean, no one is free to dictate to the ICBI framers what they meant by inerrancy. This is particularly true of those who subscribe to the grammatical-historical method of interpretation, as the ICBI framers did. For if a document should be interpreted in accord with the expressed intentions of an author, then there are stated limits (as shown above) on what inerrancy does or does not cover.

Failing to follow this path gave rise to an acute problem in the Evangelical Theological Society (ETS). The issue surfaced in 1976 when the ETS Executive Committee confessed that "Some of the members of the Society have expressed the feeling that a measure of **intellectual dishonesty prevails among members who do not take the signing of the doctrinal statement seriously.**" Other "members of the Society have come to the realization that they are not in agreement with the creedal statement and have voluntarily withdrawn. That is, **in good conscience** they could not sign the statement" (1976 ETS Minutes, emphasis added). Later, (in 1983 ETS minutes) an ETS Ad Hoc Committee recognized this problem when it posed the proper question: "**Is it acceptable for a member of the society to hold a view of biblical author's intent which disagrees with the Founding Fathers and even the majority of the society, and still remain a member in good standing?**" Failing to say "No" is not only contrary to the expressed "intention of the author" view, but it opens the door for a deconstructionist and reconstructionist view of doctrinal statements like those of the ICBI. It is hoped that these primary ICBI sources contained in this book can help avoid this problem among those who claim to subscribe to biblical inerrancy. Since the three living framers of the ICBI statements (Sproul, Packer, and I)[5] concur on these matters, it would be as presumptuous to reject this official understanding of the ICBI statement on these matter as it would be for a liberal judge to reject the meaning of Thomas Jefferson, James Madison, and John Adams on the First Amendment to the U.S. Constitution.[6]

Dr. Norman L. Geisler
January 28th, 2013
Matthews, North Carolina

1. See Norman L. Geisler and William C. Roach, *Defending Inerrancy: Affirming the Accuracy of Scripture for a New Generation* (Grand Rapids: Baker Books, 2011). Also see http://defendinginerrancy.com.
2. R.C. Sproul, *Explaining Inerrancy: A Commentary* (ICBI, 1980), 43-44. Also R.C. Sproul, "Book IV: Explaining Inerrancy: A Commentary on the Chicago Statement," in *Explaining Biblical Inerrancy* (Bastion Books, 2013), 110.
3. Also see "Genre Criticism," in *Hermeneutics, Inerrancy and The Bible*. Eds. Earl D. Radmacher and Robert D. Preus (Grand Rapids: Zondervan, 1984) 165-216.
4. I first addressed this issue in *The Journal of the Evangelical Theological Society* (JETS) in 1983. See https://www.etsjets.org or http://normangeisler.com/methodological-unorthodoxy
5. All three of these "living framers" proceeded to pass into eternity within the next seven years—Robert Charles Sproul (1939-2017), Norman Leo Geisler (1932-2019), and James Innell Packer (1926-2020). Further elaboration on their concurrence "on these matters" between 2011 and 2014 may be found in Norman Geisler, *Preserving Orthodoxy: Maintaining Continuity with the Historic Christian Faith on Scripture* (Bastion Books, 2017) 104-109. - C.T.H., July 2021
6. For the sake of historical accuracy, it seems that James Madison was the sole author of the First Amendment to the U.S. Constitution. Neither Thomas Jefferson nor John Adams appear to have contributed directly to its wording. However, Jefferson may have influenced—or perhaps even guided—Madison on these matters. If so, Jefferson's contribution to the amendment, while indirect, was quite significant. He could have served as an able spokesman for it. As for John Adams, even though he may not have contributed to the amendment, he nevertheless demonstrated support for its principles and would have probably made a good spokesman for it too. The qualifications for R.C. Sproul, J.I. Packer, and Norm Geisler to serve as spokesmen for the articles of the Chicago Statement on Biblical Inerrancy (CSBI) are even stronger in this analogy. In concert with one another, and with others in the ICBI, these "last living framers" all contributed to the wording of the articles back in 1978. As a result, they would have been not just the last but the best-qualified commentators to clarify in the early 2010s what kinds of interpretive practices those articles—both in letter and in spirit—were intended to encourage or discourage. – C.T.H., July 2021

BOOK I

CSBI

THE CHICAGO STATEMENT ON BIBLICAL INERRANCY

Copyright © 1978
The International Council on Biblical Inerrancy
All rights reserved.

INTRODUCTION

The authority of Scripture is a key issue for the Christian Church in this and every age. Those who profess faith in Jesus Christ as Lord and Savior are called to show the reality of their discipleship by humbly and faithfully obeying God's written Word. To stray from Scripture in faith or conduct is disloyalty to our Master. Recognition of the total truth and trustworthiness of Holy Scripture is essential to a full grasp and adequate confession of its authority.

The following Statement affirms this inerrancy of Scripture afresh, making clear our understanding of it and warning against its denial. We are persuaded that to deny it is to set aside the witness of Jesus Christ and of the Holy Spirit and to refuse that submission to the claims of God's own Word which marks true Christian faith. We see it as our timely, duty to make this affirmation in the face of current lapses from the truth of inerrancy among our fellow Christians and misunderstanding of this doctrine in the world at large.

This Statement consists of three parts: a Summary Statement, Articles of Affirmation and Denial, and an accompanying Exposition. It has been prepared in the course of a three-day consultation in Chicago. Those who have signed the Summary Statement and the

Articles wish to affirm their own conviction as to the inerrancy of Scripture and to encourage and challenge one another and all Christians to growing appreciation and understanding of this doctrine. We acknowledge the limitations of a document prepared in a brief, intensive conference and do not propose that this Statement be given creedal weight. Yet we rejoice in the deepening of our own convictions through our discussions together, and we pray that the Statement we have signed may be used to the glory of our God toward a new reformation of the Church in its faith, life, and mission.

We offer this Statement in a spirit, not of contention, but of humility and love, which we purpose by God's grace to maintain in any future dialogue arising out of what we have said. We gladly acknowledge that many who deny the inerrancy of Scripture do not display the consequences of this denial in the rest of their belief and behavior, and we are conscious that we who confess this doctrine often deny it in life by failing to bring our thoughts and deeds, our traditions and habits, into true subjection to the divine Word.

We invite response to this statement from any who see reason to amend its affirmations about Scripture by the light of Scripture itself, under whose infallible authority we stand as we speak. We claim no personal infallibility for the witness we bear, and for any help which enables us to strengthen this testimony to God's Word we shall be grateful.

The Draft Committee

A SHORT STATEMENT

1. God, who is Himself Truth and speaks truth only, has inspired Holy Scripture in order thereby to reveal Himself to lost mankind through Jesus Christ as Creator and Lord, Redeemer and Judge. Holy Scripture is God's witness to Himself.
2. Holy Scripture, being God's own Word, written by men prepared and superintended by His Spirit, is of infallible divine authority in all matters upon which it touches: it is to be believed, as God's instruction, in all that it affirms; obeyed, as God's command, in all that it requires; embraced, as God's pledge, in all that it promises.
3. The Holy Spirit, Scripture's divine Author, both authenticates it to us by His inward witness and opens our minds to understand its meaning.
4. Being wholly and verbally God-given, Scripture is without error or fault in all its teaching, no less in what it states about God's acts in creation, about the events of world history, and about its own literary origins under God, than in its witness to God's saving grace in individual lives.
5. The authority of Scripture is inescapably impaired if this

total divine inerrancy is in any way limited or disregarded, or made relative to a view of truth contrary to the Bible's own; and such lapses bring serious loss to both the individual and the Church.

Articles of Affirmations and Denials

Article I

We affirm that the Holy Scriptures are to be received as the authoritative Word of God.

We deny that the Scriptures receive their authority from the church, tradition or any other human source.

Article II

We affirm that the Scriptures are the supreme written norm by which God binds the conscience, and that the authority of the church is subordinate to that of Scripture.

We deny that church creeds, councils or declarations have authority greater than or equal to the authority of the Bible.

Article III

We affirm that the written Word in its entirety is revelation given by God.

We deny that the Bible is merely a witness to revelation, or only becomes revelation in encounter, or depends on the responses of men for its validity.

Article IV

We affirm that God who made mankind in his image has used language as a means of revelation.

We deny that human language is so limited by our creatureliness that it is rendered inadequate as a vehicle for divine revelation. **We further deny** that the corruption of human culture and language through sin has thwarted God's work of inspiration.

Article V

We affirm that God's revelation in the Holy Scriptures was progressive.

We deny that later revelation, which may fulfill earlier revelation, ever corrects or contradicts it. **We further deny** that any normative revelation has been given since the completion of the New Testament writings.

Article VI

We affirm that the whole of Scripture and all its parts, down to the very words of the original, were given by divine inspiration.

We deny that the inspiration of Scripture can rightly be affirmed of the whole without the parts, or of some parts but not the whole.

Article VII

We affirm that inspiration was the work in which God by His Spirit, through human writers, gave us His Word. The origin of Scripture is divine. The mode of divine inspiration remains largely a mystery to us.

We deny that inspiration can be reduced to human insight, or to heightened states of consciousness of any kind.

Article VIII

We affirm that God in His work of inspiration utilized the distinctive personalities and literary styles of the writers whom He had chosen and prepared.

We deny that God, in causing these writers to use the very words that He chose, overrode their personalities.

Article IX

We affirm that inspiration, though not conferring omniscience, guaranteed true and trustworthy utterance on all matters of which the biblical authors were moved to speak and write.

We deny that the finitude or fallenness of these writers, by necessity or otherwise, introduced distortion or falsehood into God's Word.

Article X

We affirm that inspiration, strictly speaking, applies only to the autographic text of Scripture, which in the providence of God can be ascertained from available manuscripts with great accuracy. **We further affirm** that copies and translations of Scripture are the Word of God to the extent that they faithfully represent the original.

We deny that any essential element of the Christian faith is affected by the absence of the autographs. We further deny that this absence renders the assertion of biblical inerrancy invalid or irrelevant.

Article XI

We affirm that Scripture, having been given by divine inspiration, is infallible, so that, far from misleading us, it is true and reliable in all the matters it addresses.

We deny that it is possible for the Bible to be at the same time infallible and errant in its assertions. Infallibility and inerrancy may be distinguished, but not separated.

Article XII

We affirm that Scripture in its entirety is inerrant, being free from all falsehood, fraud or deceit.

We deny that biblical infallibility and inerrancy are limited to spiritual, religious or redemptive themes, exclusive of assertions in the fields of history and science. We further deny that scientific hypotheses about earth history may properly be used to overturn the teaching of Scripture on creation and the flood.

Article XIII

We affirm the propriety of using inerrancy as a theological term with reference to the complete truthfulness of Scripture.

We deny that it is proper to evaluate Scripture according to standards of truth and error that are alien to its usage or purpose. We further deny that inerrancy is negated by biblical phenomena such as a lack of modern technical precision, irregularities of grammar or spelling, observational descriptions of nature, the reporting of falsehoods, the use of hyperbole and round numbers, the topical arrangement of material, variant selections of material in parallel accounts, or the use of free citations.

Article XIV

We affirm the unity and internal consistency of Scripture.

We deny that alleged errors and discrepancies that have not yet been resolved vitiate the truth claims of the Bible.

Article XV

We affirm that the doctrine of inerrancy is grounded in the teaching of the Bible about inspiration.

We deny that Jesus' teaching about Scripture may be dismissed by appeals to accommodation or to any natural limitation of His humanity.

Article XVI

We affirm that the doctrine of inerrancy has been integral to the Church's faith throughout its history.

We deny that inerrancy is a doctrine invented by Scholastic Protestantism, or is a reactionary position postulated in response to negative higher criticism.

Article XVII

We affirm that the Holy Spirit bears witness to the Scriptures, assuring believers of the truthfulness of God's written Word.

We deny that this witness of the Holy Spirit operates in isolation from or against Scripture.

Article XVIII

We affirm that the text of Scripture is to be interpreted by grammatico-historical exegesis, taking account of its literary forms and devices, and that Scripture is to interpret Scripture.

We deny the legitimacy of any treatment of the text or quest for sources lying behind it that leads to relativizing, dehistoricizing, or discounting its teaching, or rejecting its claims to authorship.

Article XIX

We affirm that a confession of the full authority, infallibility and inerrancy of Scripture is vital to a sound understanding of the whole of the Christian faith. **We further affirm** that such confession should lead to increasing conformity to the image of Christ.

We deny that such confession is necessary for salvation. However, **we further deny** that inerrancy can be rejected without grave consequences, both to the individual and to the church.

EXPOSITION

Our understanding of the doctrine of inerrancy must be set in the context of the broader teachings of the Scripture concerning itself. This exposition gives an account of the outline of doctrine from which our summary statement and articles are drawn.

CREATION, REVELATION, AND INSPIRATION

The Triune God, who formed all things by his creative utterances and governs all things by His Word of decree, made mankind in His own image for a life of communion with Himself, on the model of the eternal fellowship of loving communication within the Godhead. As God's image-bearer, man was to hear God's Word addressed to him and to respond in the joy of adoring obedience. Over and above God's self-disclosure in the created order and the sequence of events within it, human beings from Adam on have received verbal messages from Him, either directly, as stated in Scripture, or indirectly in the form of part or all of Scripture itself.

When Adam fell, the Creator did not abandon mankind to final judgment but promised salvation and began to reveal Himself as

Redeemer in a sequence of historical events centering on Abraham's family and culminating in the life, death, resurrection, present heavenly ministry, and promised return of Jesus Christ. Within this frame God has from time to time spoken specific words of judgment and mercy, promise and command, to sinful human beings so drawing them into a covenant relation of mutual commitment between Him and them in which He blesses them with gifts of grace and they bless Him in responsive adoration. Moses, whom God used as mediator to carry His words to His people at the time of the Exodus, stands at the head of a long line of prophets in whose mouths and writings God put His words for delivery to Israel. God's purpose in this succession of messages was to maintain His covenant by causing His people to know His Name - that is, His nature - and His will both of precept and purpose in the present and for the future. This line of prophetic spokesmen from God came to completion in Jesus Christ, God's incarnate Word, who was Himself a prophet - more than a prophet, but not less - and in the apostles and prophets of the first Christian generation. When God's final and climactic message, His word to the world concerning Jesus Christ, had been spoken and elucidated by those in the apostolic circle, the sequence of revealed messages ceased. Henceforth the Church was to live and know God by what He had already said, and said for all time.

At Sinai God wrote the terms of His covenant on tables of stone, as His enduring witness and for lasting - accessibility: and throughout the period of prophetic and apostolic revelation He prompted men to write the messages given to and through them, along with celebratory records of His dealings with His people, plus moral reflections on covenant life and forms of praise and prayer for covenant mercy. The theological reality of inspiration in the producing of Biblical documents corresponds to that of spoken prophecies: although the human writers' personalities were expressed in what they wrote, the words were divinely constituted. Thus, what Scripture says, God says; its authority is His authority, for He is its ultimate Author, having given it through the minds and words of chosen and prepared men who in freedom and faithfulness "spoke from God as they were carried along by the Holy Spirit" (1 Pet. 1:21). Holy Scripture must be acknowledged as the Word of God by virtue of its divine origin.

AUTHORITY: CHRIST AND THE BIBLE

Jesus Christ, the Son of God who is the Word made flesh, our Prophet, Priest, and King, is the ultimate Mediator of God's communication to man, as He is of all God's gifts of grace. The revelation He gave was more than verbal; He revealed the Father by His presence and His deeds as well. Yet His words were crucially important; for He was God, He spoke from the Father, and His words will judge all men at the last day.

As the prophesied Messiah, Jesus Christ is the central theme of Scripture. The Old Testament looked ahead to Him; the New Testament looks back to His first coming and on to His second. Canonical Scripture is the divinely inspired and therefore normative witness to Christ. No hermeneutic, therefore, of which the historical Christ is not the focal point is acceptable. Holy Scripture must be treated as what it essentially is - the witness of the Father to the incarnate Son.

It appears that the Old Testament canon had been fixed by the time of Jesus. The New Testament canon is likewise now closed inasmuch as no new apostolic witness to the historical Christ can now be borne. No new revelation (as distinct from Spirit-given understanding of existing revelation) will be given until Christ comes again. The canon was created in principle by divine inspiration. The Church's part was to discern the canon which God had created, not to devise one of its own.

The word *canon*, signifying a rule or standard, is a pointer to authority, which means the right to rule and control. Authority in Christianity belongs to God in His revelation, which means, on the one hand, Jesus Christ, the living Word, and, on the other hand, Holy Scripture, the written Word. But the authority of Christ and that of Scripture are one. As our Prophet, Christ testified that Scripture cannot be broken. As our Priest and King, He devoted His earthly life to fulfilling the law and the prophets, even dying in obedience to the words of Messianic prophecy. Thus, as He saw Scripture attesting Him and His authority, so by His own submission to Scripture He attested its authority. As He bowed to His Father's instruction given in His Bible (our Old Testament), so He requires His disciples to do - not, however, in isolation but in conjunction with the apostolic witness to Himself which He undertook to inspire by His gift of the Holy Spirit. So Christians show themselves faithful servants of their Lord by bowing to the divine instruction given in the prophetic and apostolic writings which together make up our Bible.

By authenticating each other's authority, Christ and Scripture coalesce into a single fount of authority. The Biblically-interpreted Christ and the Christ-centered, Christ-proclaiming Bible are from this standpoint one. As from the fact of inspiration we infer that what Scripture says, God says, so from the revealed relation between Jesus Christ and Scripture we may equally declare that what Scripture says, Christ says.

INFALLIBILITY, INERRANCY, INTERPRETATION

Holy Scripture, as the inspired Word of God witnessing authoritatively to Jesus Christ, may properly be called *infallible* and *inerrant*. These negative terms have a special value, for they explicitly safeguard crucial positive truths.

Infallible signifies the quality of neither misleading nor being misled and so safeguards in categorical terms the truth that Holy Scripture is a sure, safe, and reliable rule and guide in all matters.

Similarly, *inerrant* signifies the quality of being free from all falsehood or mistake and so safeguards the truth that Holy Scripture is entirely true and trustworthy in all its assertions.

We affirm that canonical Scripture should always be interpreted on the basis that it is infallible and inerrant. However, in determining what the God-taught writer is asserting in each passage, we must pay the most careful attention to its claims and character as a human production. In inspiration, God utilized the culture and conventions of his penman's milieu, a milieu that God controls in His sovereign providence; it is misinterpretation to imagine otherwise.

So history must be treated as history, poetry as poetry, hyperbole and metaphor as hyperbole and metaphor, generalization and approximation as what they are, and so forth. Differences between literary conventions in Bible times and in ours must also be observed: since, for instance, non-chronological narration and imprecise citation were conventional and acceptable and violated no expectations in those days, we must not regard these things as faults when we find them in Bible writers. When total precision of a particular kind was not expected nor aimed at, it is no error not to have achieved it. Scripture is inerrant, not in the sense of being absolutely precise by modern standards, but in the sense of making good its claims and achieving that measure of focused truth at which its authors aimed.

The truthfulness of Scripture is not negated by the appearance in it of irregularities of grammar or spelling, phenomenal descriptions of nature, reports of false statements (*e.g.*, the lies of Satan), or seeming discrepancies between one passage and another. It is not right to set the so-called "phenomena" of Scripture against the teaching of Scripture about itself. Apparent inconsistencies should not be ignored. Solution of them, where this can be convincingly achieved, will encourage our faith, and where for the present no convincing solution is at hand we shall significantly honor God by trusting His assurance that His Word is true, despite these appearances, and by maintaining our confidence that one day they will be seen to have been illusions.

Inasmuch as all Scripture is the product of a single divine mind, interpretation must stay within the bounds of the analogy of Scripture and eschew hypotheses that would correct one Biblical passage by another, whether in the name of progressive revelation or of the imperfect enlightenment of the inspired writer's mind.

Although Holy Scripture is nowhere culture-bound in the sense that its teaching lacks universal validity, it is sometimes culturally conditioned by the customs and conventional views of a particular period, so that the application of its principles today calls for a different sort of action.

SKEPTICISM AND CRITICISM

Since the Renaissance, and more particularly since the Enlightenment, world-views have been developed which involve skepticism about basic Christian tenets. Such are the agnosticism which denies that -God is knowable, the rationalism which denies that He is incomprehensible, the idealism which denies that He is transcendent, and the existentialism which denies rationality in His relationships with us. When these un- and anti-biblical principles seep into men's theologies at presuppositional level, as today they frequently do, faithful interpretation of Holy Scripture becomes impossible.

TRANSMISSION AND TRANSLATION

Since God has nowhere promised an inerrant transmission of Scripture, it is necessary to affirm that only the autographic text of the original documents was inspired and to maintain the need of textual criticism as a means of detecting any slips that may have crept into the text in the course of its transmission. The verdict of this science, however, is that the Hebrew and Greek text appear to be amazingly well preserved, so that we are amply justified in affirming, with the

Westminster Confession, a singular providence of God in this matter and in declaring that the authority of Scripture is in no way jeopardized by the fact that the copies we possess are not entirely error-free.

Similarly, no translation is or can be perfect, and all translations are an additional step away from the *autographa*. Yet the verdict of linguistic science is that English-speaking Christians, at least, are exceedingly well served in these days with a host of excellent translations and have no cause for hesitating to conclude that the true Word of God is within their reach. Indeed, in view of the frequent repetition in Scripture of the main matters with which it deals and also of the Holy Spirit's constant witness to and through the Word, no serious translation of Holy Scripture will so destroy its meaning as to render it unable to make its reader "wise for salvation through faith in Christ Jesus" (2Tim.3:15).

INERRANCY AND AUTHORITY

In our affirmation of the authority of Scripture as involving its total truth, we are consciously standing with Christ and His apostles, indeed with the whole Bible and with the main stream of Church history from the first days until very recently. We are concerned at the casual, inadvertent, and seemingly thoughtless way in which a belief of such far-reaching importance has been given up by so many in our day.

We are conscious too that great and grave confusion results from ceasing to maintain the total truth of the Bible whose authority one professes to acknowledge. The result of taking this step is that the Bible which God gave loses its authority, and what has authority instead is a Bible reduced in content according to the demands of one's critical reasonings and in principle reducible still further once one has started. This means that at bottom independent reason now has authority, as opposed to Scriptural teaching. If this is not seen and if for the time being basic evangelical doctrines are still held, persons denying the full truth of Scripture may claim an evangelical identity while methodologically they have moved away from the evangelical principle of knowledge to an unstable subjectivism, and will find it hard not to move further.

We affirm that what Scripture says, God says. May He be glorified. Amen and Amen.

BOOK II

CSBH

THE CHICAGO STATEMENT ON BIBLICAL HERMENEUTICS

Copyright © 1982
The International Council on Biblical Inerrancy
All rights reserved.

INTRODUCTION

Summit I of the International Council on Biblical Inerrancy took place in Chicago on October 26-28, 1978 for the purpose of affirming afresh the doctrine of the inerrancy of Scripture, making clear the understanding of it and warning against its denial. In the seven years since Summit I, God has blessed that effort in ways surpassing most anticipations. A gratifying show of helpful literature on the doctrine of inerrancy as well as a growing commitment to its value give cause to pour forth praise to our great God.

The work of Summit I had hardly been completed when it became evident that there was yet another major task to be tackled. While we recognize that belief in the inerrancy of Scripture is basic to maintaining its authority, the values of that commitment are only as real as one's understanding of the meaning of Scripture. Thus, the need for Summit II. For two years plans were laid and papers were written on themes relating to hermeneutical principles and practices. The culmination of this effort has been a meeting in Chicago on November 10-13, 1982 at which we, the undersigned, have participated.

In similar fashion to the Chicago Statement of 1978, we herewith present these affirmations and denials as an expression of the results of our labors to clarify hermeneutical issues and principles. We do not claim completeness or systematic treatment of the entire subject, but these affirmations and denials represent a consensus of the approximately one hundred participants and observers gathered at this conference. It has been a broadening experience to engage in dialogue, and it is our prayer that God will use the product of our diligent efforts to enable us and others to more correctly handle the word of truth (2 Tim. 2:15).

ARTICLES OF AFFIRMATION AND DENIAL

Article I

We affirm that the normative authority of Holy Scripture is the authority of God Himself, and is attested by Jesus Christ, the Lord of the Church.

We deny the legitimacy of separating the authority of Christ from the authority of Scripture, or of opposing the one to the other.

Article II

We affirm that as Christ is God and Man in one Person, so Scripture is, indivisibly, God's Word in human language.

We deny that the humble, human form of Scripture entails errancy any more than the humanity of Christ, even in His humiliation, entails sin.

Article III

We affirm that the person and work of Jesus Christ are the central focus of the entire Bible.

We deny that any method of interpretation which rejects or obscures the Christ-centeredness of Scripture is correct.

Article IV

We affirm that the Holy Spirit who inspired Scripture acts through it today to work faith in its message.

We deny that the Holy Spirit ever teaches to any one anything which is contrary to the teaching of Scripture.

Article V

We affirm that the Holy Spirit enables believers to appropriate and apply Scripture to their lives.

We deny that the natural man is able to discern spiritually the biblical message apart from the Holy Spirit.

Article VI

We affirm that the Bible expresses God's truth in propositional statements, and we declare that biblical truth is both objective and absolute. We further affirm that a statement is true if it represents matters as they actually are, but is an error if it misrepresents the facts.

We deny that, while Scripture is able to make us wise unto salvation, biblical truth should be defined in terms of this function. We further deny that error should be defined as that which willfully deceives.

Article VII

We affirm that the meaning expressed in each biblical text is single, definite, and fixed.

We deny that the recognition of this single meaning eliminates the variety of its application.

Article VIII

We affirm that the Bible contains teachings and mandates which apply to all cultural and situational contexts and other mandates which the Bible itself shows apply only to particular situations.

We deny that the distinction between the universal and particular mandates of Scripture can be determined by cultural and situational factors. We further deny that universal mandates may ever be treated as culturally or situationally relative.

Article IX

We affirm that the term hermeneutics, which historically signified the rules of exegesis, may properly be extended to cover all that is involved in the process of perceiving what the biblical revelation means and how it bears on our lives.

We deny that the message of Scripture derives from, or is dictated by, the interpreter's understanding. Thus we deny that the "horizons" of the biblical writer and the interpreter may rightly "fuse" in such a way that what the text communicates to the interpreter is not ultimately controlled by the expressed meaning of the Scripture.

Article X

We affirm that Scripture communicates God's truth to us verbally through a wide variety of literary forms.

We deny that any of the limits of human language render Scripture inadequate to convey God's message.

Article XI

We affirm that translations of the text of Scripture can communicate knowledge of God across all temporal and cultural boundaries.

We deny that the meaning of biblical texts is so tied to the culture out of which they came that understanding of the same meaning in other cultures is impossible.

Article XII

We affirm that in the task of translating the Bible and teaching it in the context of each culture, only those functional equivalents that are faithful to the content of biblical teaching should be employed.

We deny the legitimacy of methods which either are insensitive to the demands of cross-cultural communication or distort biblical meaning in the process.

Article XIII

We affirm that awareness of the literary categories, formal and stylistic, of the various parts of Scripture is essential for proper exegesis, and hence we value genre criticism as one of the many disciplines of biblical study.

We deny that generic categories which negate historicity may rightly be imposed on biblical narratives which present themselves as factual.

Article XIV

We affirm that the biblical record of events, discourses and sayings, though presented in a variety of appropriate literary forms, corresponds to historical fact.

We deny that any such event, discourse or saying reported in Scripture was invented by the biblical writers or by the traditions they incorporated.

Article XV

We affirm the necessity of interpreting the Bible according to its literal, or normal, sense. The literal sense is the grammatical-historical sense, that is, the meaning which the writer expressed. Interpretation according to the literal sense will take account of all figures of speech and literary forms found in the text.

We deny the legitimacy of any approach to Scripture that attributes to it meaning which the literal sense does not support.

Article XVI

We affirm that legitimate critical techniques should be used in determining the canonical text and its meaning.

We deny the legitimacy of allowing any method of biblical criticism to question the truth or integrity of the writer's expressed meaning, or of any other scriptural teaching.

Article XVII

We affirm the unity, harmony, and consistency of Scripture and declare that it is its own best interpreter.

We deny that Scripture may be interpreted in such a way as to suggest that one passage corrects or militates against another. We deny that later writers of Scripture misinterpreted earlier passages of Scripture when quoting from or referring to them.

Article XVIII

We affirm that the Bible's own interpretation of itself is always correct, never deviating from, but rather elucidating, the single meaning of the inspired text. The single meaning of a prophet's words includes, but is not restricted to, the understanding of those words by the prophet and necessarily involves the intention of God evidenced in the fulfillment of those words.

We deny that the writers of Scripture always understood the full implications of their own words.

Article XIX

We affirm that any preunderstandings which the interpreter brings to Scripture should be in harmony with scriptural teaching and subject to correction by it.

We deny that Scripture should be required to fit alien preunderstandings, inconsistent with itself, such as naturalism, evolutionism, scientism, secular humanism, and relativism.

Article XX

We affirm that since God is the author of all truth, all truths, biblical and extrabiblical, are consistent and cohere, and that the Bible speaks truth when it touches on matters pertaining to nature, history, or anything else. We further affirm that in some cases extrabiblical data have value for clarifying what Scripture teaches, and for prompting correction of faulty interpretations.

We deny that extrabiblical views ever disprove the teaching of Scripture or hold priority over it.

Article XXI

We affirm the harmony of special with general revelation and therefore of biblical teaching with the facts of nature.

We deny that any genuine scientific facts are inconsistent with the true meaning of any passage of Scripture.

Article XXII

We affirm that Genesis 1-11 is factual, as is the rest of the book.

We deny that the teachings of Genesis 1-11 are mythical and that scientific hypotheses about earth history or the origin of humanity may be invoked to overthrow what Scripture teaches about creation.

Article XXIII

We affirm the clarity of Scripture and specifically of its message about salvation from sin.

We deny that all passages of Scripture are equally clear or have equal bearing on the message of redemption.

Article XXIV

We affirm that a person is not dependent for understanding of Scripture on the expertise of biblical scholars.

We deny that a person should ignore the fruits of the technical study of Scripture by biblical scholars.

Article XXV

We affirm that the only type of preaching which sufficiently conveys the divine revelation and its proper application to life is that which faithfully expounds the text of Scripture as the Word of God.

We deny that the preacher has any message from God apart from the text of Scripture.

EXPOSITION

The following paragraphs outline the general theological understanding which the Chicago Statement on Biblical Hermeneutics reflects. They were first drafted as a stimulus toward that statement. They have now been revised in the light of it and of many specific suggestions received during the scholars' conference at which it was drawn up. Though the revision could not be completed in time to present to the conference, there is every reason to regard its substance as expressing with broad accuracy the common mind of the signatories of the statement.

Standpoint of the Exposition

The living God, Creator and Redeemer, is a communicator, and the inspired and inerrant Scriptures which set before us his saving revelation in history are his means of communicating with us today. He who once spoke to the world through Jesus Christ his Son speaks to us still in and through his written Word. Publicly and privately, therefore, through preaching, personal study and meditation, with prayer and in the fellowship of the body of Christ, Christian people must continually labor to interpret the Scriptures so that their normative divine message to us may be properly understood. To have formulated the biblical concept of Scripture as authoritative revelation in writing, the God-given rule of faith and life, will be of no profit where the message of Scripture is not rightly grasped and applied. So it is of vital importance to detect and dismiss defective ways of interpreting what is written and to replace them with faithful interpretation of God's infallible Word.

That is the purpose this exposition seeks to serve. What it offers is basic perspectives on the hermeneutical task in the light of three convictions. First, Scripture, being God's own instruction to us, is abidingly true and utterly trustworthy. Second, hermeneutics is crucial to the battle for biblical authority in the contemporary church. Third, as knowledge of the inerrancy of Scripture must control interpretation, forbidding us to discount anything that Scripture proves to affirm, so interpretation must clarify the scope and significance of that inerrancy by determining what affirmations Scripture actually makes.

The Communion between God and Mankind

God has made mankind in his own image, personal and rational, for eternal loving fellowship with himself in a communion that rests on two-way communication: God addressing to us words of revelation and we answering him in words of prayer and praise. God's gift of language was given us partly to make possible these interchanges and partly also that we might share our understanding of God with others.

In testifying to the historical process from Adam to Christ whereby God re-established fellowship with our fallen race, Scripture depicts him as constantly using his own gift of language to send men messages about what he would do and what they should do. The God of the Bible uses many forms of speech: he narrates, informs, instructs, warns, reasons, promises, commands, explains, exclaims, entreats and encourages. The God who saves is also the God who speaks in all these ways.

Biblical writers, historians, prophets, poets and teachers alike, cite Scripture as God's word of address to all its readers and hearers. To regard Scripture as the Creator's present personal invitation to fellowship, setting standards for faith and godliness not only for its own time but for all time, is integral to biblical faith.

Though God is revealed in the natural order, in the course of history and in the deliverances of conscience, sin makes mankind impervious and unresponsive to this general revelation. And general revelation is in any case only a disclosure of the Creator as the world's good Lord and just Judge; it does not tell of salvation through Jesus Christ. To know about the Christ of Scripture is thus a necessity for that knowledge of God and communion with him to which he calls sinners today. As the biblical message is heard, read, preached and taught, the Holy Spirit works with and through it to open the eyes of the spiritually blind and to instill this knowledge.

God has caused Scripture so to be written, and the Spirit so ministers with it, that all who read it, humbly seeking God's help, will be able to understand its saving message. The Spirit's ministry does not make needless the discipline of personal study but rather makes it effective.

To deny the rational, verbal, cognitive character of God's communication to us, to posit an antithesis as some do between revelation as personal and as propositional, and to doubt the adequacy of language as we have It to bring us God's authentic message are fundamental mistakes. The humble verbal form of biblical language no more invalidates it as revelation of God's mind than the humble servant-form of the Word made flesh invalidates the claim that Jesus truly reveals the Father.

To deny that God has made plain in Scripture as much as each human being needs to know for his or her spiritual welfare would be a further mistake. Any obscurities we find in Scripture are not intrinsic to it but reflect our own limitations of information and insight. Scripture is clear and sufficient both as a source of doctrine, binding the conscience, and as a guide to eternal life and godliness, shaping our worship and service of the God who creates, loves and saves.

The Authority of Scripture

Holy Scripture is the self-revelation of God in and through the words of men. It is both their witness to God and God's witness to himself. As the divine-human record and interpretation of God's redemptive work in history, it is cognitive revelation, truth addressed to our minds for understanding and response. God is its source, and Jesus Christ, the Savior, is its center of reference and main subject matter. Its absolute and abiding worth as an infallible directive for faith and living follows from its God-givenness (cf. 2 Tim. 3:15-17). Being as fully divine as it is human, it expresses God's wisdom in all its teaching and speaks reliably — that is, infallibly and inerrantly—in every informative assertion it makes, It is a set of occasional writings, each with its own specific character and content, which together constitute an organism of universally relevant truth, namely, bad news about universal human sin and need answered by good news about a particular first-century Jew who is shown to be the Son of God and the world's only Savior. The volume which these constituent books make is as broad as life and bears upon every human problem and aspect of behavior. In setting before us the history of redemption–the law and the gospel, God's commands, promises, threats, works and ways, and object-lessons concerning faith and obedience and their opposites, with their respective outcomes—Scripture shows us the entire panorama of human existence as God wills us to see it.

The authority of Holy Scripture is bound up with the authority of Jesus Christ, whose recorded words express the principle that the teaching of Israel's Scriptures (our Old Testament), together with his own teaching and the witness of the apostles (our New Testament), constitute his appointed rule of faith and conduct for his followers. He did not criticize his Bible, though he criticized misinterpretations of it; on the contrary, he affirmed its binding authority over him and all his disciples (cf. Matt. 5:17-19). To separate the authority of Christ from that of Scripture and to oppose the one to the other are thus mistakes. To oppose the authority of one apostle to that of another or the teaching of an apostle at one time to that of his teaching at another time are mistakes also.

The Holy Spirit and the Scriptures

The Holy Spirit of God, who moved the human authors to produce the biblical books, now accompanies them with his power. He led the church to discern their inspiration in the canonizing process; he continually confirms this discernment to individuals through the unique impact which he causes Scripture to make upon them. He helps them as they study, pray, meditate and seek to learn in the church, to understand and commit themselves to those things which the Bible teaches, and to know the living triune God whom the Bible presents.

The Spirit's illumination can only be expected where the biblical text is diligently studied. Illumination does not yield new truth, over and above what the Bible says; rather, it enables us to see what Scripture was showing us all along. Illumination binds our consciences to Scripture as God's Word and brings joy and worship as we find the Word yielding up to us its meaning. By contrast, intellectual and emotional impulses to disregard or quarrel with the teaching of Scripture come not from the Spirit of God but from some other source. Demonstrable misunderstandings and misinterpretations of Scripture may not be ascribed to the Spirit's leading.

The Idea of Hermeneutics

Biblical hermeneutics has traditionally been understood as the study of right principles for understanding the biblical text. "Understanding" may stop short at a theoretical and notional level, or it may advance via the assent and commitment of faith to become experiential through personal acquaintance with the God to whom the theories and notions refer. Theoretical understanding of Scripture requires of us no more than is called for to comprehend any ancient literature, that is, sufficient knowledge of the language and background and sufficient empathy with the different cultural context. But there is no experiential understanding of Scripture — no personal knowledge of the God to whom it points — without the Spirit's illumination. Biblical hermeneutics studies the way in which both levels of understanding are attained.

The Scope of Biblical Interpretation

The interpreter's task in broadest definition is to understand both what Scripture meant historically and what it means for us today, that is, how it bears on our lives. This task involves three constant activities.

First comes *exegesis*, this extracting from the text of what God by the human writer was expressing to the latter's envisaged readers.

Second comes *integration*, the correlating of what each exegetical venture has yielded with whatever other biblical teaching bears on the matter in hand and with the rest of biblical teaching as such. Only within this frame of reference can the full meaning of the exegeted teaching be determined.

Third comes *application* of the exegeted teaching, viewed explicitly as God's teaching, for the correcting and directing of thought and action. Application is based on the knowledge that God's character and will, man's nature and need, the saving ministry of Jesus Christ, the experiential aspects of godliness including the common life of the church and the many-sided relationship between God and his world including his plan for its history are realities which do not change with the passing years. It is with these matters that both testaments constantly deal.

Interpretation and application of Scripture take place most naturally in preaching, and all preaching should be based on this threefold procedure. Otherwise, biblical teaching will be misunderstood and misapplied, and confusion and ignorance regarding God and his ways will result.

Formal Rules of Biblical Interpretation

The faithful use of reason in biblical interpretation is ministerial, not magisterial; the believing interpreter will use his mind not to impose or manufacture meaning but to grasp the meaning that is already there in the material itself. The work of scholars who, though not themselves Christians, have been able to understand biblical ideas accurately will be a valuable resource in the theoretical part of the interpreter's task.

> a. Interpretation should adhere to the *literal* sense, that is, the single literary meaning which each passage carries. The initial quest is always for what God's penman meant by what he wrote. The discipline of interpretation excludes all attempts to go behind the text, just as it excludes all reading into passages of meanings which cannot be read out of them and all pursuit of ideas sparked off in us by the text which do not arise as part of the author's own expressed flow of thought. Symbols and figures of speech must be recognized for what they are, and arbitrary allegorizing (as distinct from the drawing out of typology which was demonstrably in the writer's mind) must be avoided.

b. The literal sense of each passage should be sought by the *grammatical-historical method*, that is, by asking what is the linguistically natural way to understand the text in its historical setting. Textual; historical, literary and theological study, aided by linguistic skills—philological, semantic, logical—is the way forward here. Passages should be exegeted in the context of the book of which they are part, and the quest for the writer's own meaning, as distinct from that of his known or supposed sources, must be constantly pursued. The legitimate use of the various critical disciplines is not to call into question the integrity or truth of the writer's meaning but simply to help us determine it.

c. Interpretation should adhere to the principle of *harmony* in the biblical material. Scripture exhibits a wide diversity of concepts and viewpoints within a common faith and an advancing disclosure of divine truth within the biblical period. These differences should not be minimized, but the unity which underlies the diversity should not be lost sight of at any point. We should look to Scripture to interpret Scripture and deny as a matter of method that particular texts, all of which have the one Holy Spirit as their source, can be genuinely discrepant with each other. Even when we cannot at present demonstrate their harmony in a convincing way, we should proceed on the basis that they are in fact harmonious and that fuller knowledge will show this.

d. Interpretation should be *canonical*, that is, the teaching of the Bible as a whole should always be viewed as providing the framework within which our understanding of each particular passage must finally be reached and into which it must finally be fitted.

Valuable as an aid in determining the literal meaning of biblical passages is the discipline of genre criticism, which seeks to identify in terms of style, form and content, the various literary categories to which the biblical books and particular passages within them belong. The literary genre in which each writer creates his text belongs in part at least to his own culture and will be clarified through knowledge of that culture. Since mistakes about genre lead to large-scale misunderstandings of biblical material, it is important that this particular discipline not be neglected.

The Centrality of Jesus Christ in the Biblical Message

Jesus Christ and the saving grace of God in him are the central themes of the Bible. Both Old and New Testaments bear witness to Christ, and the New Testament interpretation of the Old Testament points to him consistently. Types and prophecies in the Old Testament anticipated his coming, his atoning death, his resurrection, his reign and his return. The office and ministry of priests, prophets and kings, the divinely instituted ritual and sacrificial offerings, and the patterns of redemptive action in Old Testament history, all had typical significance as foreshadowings of Jesus. Old Testament believers looked forward to his coming and lived and were saved by faith which had Christ and his kingdom in view, just as Christians today are saved by faith in Christ, the Savior, who died for our sins and who now lives and reigns and will one day return. That the church and kingdom of Jesus Christ are central to the plan of God which Scripture reveals is not open to question, though opinions divide as to the precise way in which church and kingdom relate to each other. Any way of interpreting Scripture which misses its consistent Christ-centeredness must be judged erroneous.

Biblical and Extra-biblical Knowledge

Since all facts cohere, the truth about them must be coherent also; and since God, the author of all Scripture, is also the Lord of all facts, there can in principle be no contradiction between a right understanding of what Scripture says and a right account of any reality or event in the created order. Any appearance of contradiction here would argue misunderstanding or inadequate knowledge, either of what Scripture really affirms or of what the extra-biblical facts really are. Thus it would be a summons to reassessment and further scholarly inquiry.

Biblical Statements and Natural Science

What the Bible says about the facts of nature is as true and trustworthy as anything else it says. However, it speaks of natural phenomena as they are spoken of in ordinary language, not in the explanatory technical terms of modern science; It accounts for natural events in terms of the action of God, not in terms of causal links-within the created order; and it often describes natural processes figuratively and poetically, not analytically and prosaically as modern science seeks to do. This being so, differences of opinion as to the correct scientific account to give of natural facts and events which Scripture celebrates can hardly be avoided.

It should be-remembered, however, that Scripture was given to reveal God, not to address scientific issues in scientific terms, and that, as it does not use the language of modern science, so it does not require scientific knowledge about the internal processes of God's creation for the understanding of its essential message about God and ourselves. Scripture interprets scientific knowledge by relating it to the revealed purpose and work of God, thus establishing an ultimate context for the study and reform of scientific ideas. It is not for scientific theories to dictate what Scripture may and may not say, although extra-biblical information will sometimes helpfully expose a misinterpretation of Scripture.

In fact, interrogating biblical statements concerning nature in the light of scientific knowledge about their subject matter may help toward attaining a more precise exegesis of them. For though exegesis must be controlled by the text itself, not shaped by extraneous considerations, the exegetical process is constantly stimulated by questioning the text as to whether it means this or that.

Norm and Culture in the Biblical Revelation

As we find in Scripture unchanging truths about God and his will expressed in a variety of verbal forms, so we find them applied in a variety of cultural and situational contexts. Not all biblical teaching about conduct is normative for behavior today. Some applications of moral principles are restricted to a limited audience, the nature and extent of which Scripture itself specifies. One task of exegesis is to distinguish these absolute and normative truths from those aspects of their recorded application which are relative to changing situations. Only when this distinction is drawn can we hope to see how the same absolute truths apply to us in our own culture.

To fail to see how a particular application of an absolute principle has been culturally determined (for instance, as most would agree, Paul's command that Christians greet each other with a kiss) and to treat a revealed absolute as culturally relative (for instance, as again most would agree, God's prohibition in the Pentateuch of homosexual activity) would both be mistakes. Though cultural developments, including conventional values and latter-day social change, may legitimately challenge traditional ways of applying biblical principles, they may not be used either to modify those principles in themselves or to evade their application altogether.

In cross-cultural communication a further step must be taken, the Christian teacher must re-apply revealed absolutes to persons living in a culture that is not the teacher's own. The demands of this task highlight the importance of his being clear on what is absolute in the biblical presentation of the will and work of God and what is a culturally-relative application of it. Engaging in the task may help him toward clarity at this point by making him more alert than before to the presence in Scripture of culturally-conditioned applications of truth, which have to be adjusted according to the cultural variable.

Encountering God Through His Word

The twentieth century has seen many attempts to assert the instrumentality of Scripture in bringing to us God's Word while yet denying that that Word has been set forth for all time in the words of the biblical text. These views regard the text as the fallible human witness by means of which God fashions and prompts those insights which he gives us through preaching and Bible study. But for the most part these views include a denial that the Word of God is cognitive communication, and thus they lapse inescapably into impressionistic mysticism. Also, their denial that Scripture is the objectively given Word of God makes the relation of that Word to the text indefinable and hence permanently problematical. This is true of all current forms of neo-orthodox and existentialist theology, including the so-called "new hermeneutic," which is an extreme and incoherent version of the approach described.

The need to appreciate the cultural differences between our world and that of the biblical writers and to be ready to find that God through his Word is challenging the presuppositions and limitations of our present outlook, are two emphases currently associated with the "new hermeneutic." But both really belong to the understanding of the interpretative task which this exposition has set out.

The same is true of the emphasis laid in theology of the existentialist type on the reality of transforming encounter with God and his Son, Jesus Christ, through the Scriptures. Certainly, the crowning glory of the Scriptures is that they do in fact mediate life-giving fellowship with God incarnate, the living Christ of whom they testify, the divine Savior whose words "are spirit and are life" (John 6:63). But there is no Christ save the Christ of the Bible, and only to the extent that the Bible's presentation of Jesus and of God's plan centering upon him is trusted can genuine spiritual encounter with Jesus Christ ever be expected to take place. It is by means of disciplined interpretation of a trusted Bible that the Father and Son, through the Spirit, make themselves known to sinful men. To such transforming encounters the hermeneutical principles and procedures stated here both mark and guard the road.

James Innell Packer

BOOK III

CSBA

THE CHICAGO STATEMENT ON BIBLICAL APPLICATION

Copyright © 1986
The International Council on Biblical Inerrancy
All rights reserved.

INTRODUCTION

The International Council on Biblical Inerrancy was founded in 1977, with a planned life-span of ten years. Its goal, under God, was to seek by means of scholarly writing and teaching to restore the ebbing confidence of Christian people in the total trustworthiness of the Scriptures. Because this loss of confidence leads both to loss of clarity in stating the absolutes of authentic Christianity and to loss of muscle in maintaining them, the task was felt to be urgent. Ten years of special effort to turn the tide of uncertainty about the Bible did not seem to be too much to pledge, nor to ask the Christian public to support. In its tenth year, the Council sees what has been accomplished as cause for profound thanksgiving to God, from every point of view.

The three scholars' Summits that the Council has mounted were conceived as a logically connected series, each having a unitive as well as a consultative purpose. The 1978 Summit achieved a major restatement for our time of the historic Christian view of Holy Scripture as canonical revelation from God given in the form of composite human testimony in God's will, works and ways. The 1982 Summit reached a wide-ranging consensus on hermeneutical guidelines and controls for biblical interpretation. The 1986 Summit seeks to show the relevance of a rightly interpreted Bible to some key areas of confusion and dispute in North American culture today. The need for the second and third Summits was always clear, for confessing belief in an inerrant Bible does us little good till we know how to interpret it, and interpretation involves applying biblical truth to the realities of contemporary life.

Summit III is concerned with applying eternal truth to late twentieth-century situations. It does not highlight the evangelistic and pastoral task of ensuring that known truth is internalized and lived by, but concentrates rather on seeing what it means to live out that truth in our present-day milieu. The Summit does not center its attention on the disciplines of personal discipleship, for much good material on these exists already, and if is not here that the acutest crises of application are felt. Rather, Summit III focuses, first, on the Trinitarian foundations that must give shape to all the church's life and witness, and then on a number of community concerns that come under the heading of Christian social ethics. These themes were chosen partly for their intrinsic importance and partly because there is need to dispel doubts as to whether Bible-believers can ever agree on how to respond to them. As the consensus of Summit I dispelled doubts as to whether agreement is possible on the nature of Scripture, and the consensus of Summit II dispelled doubts as to whether inerrantists can agree on principles for interpreting the inspired text, so now Summit Ill offers a high degree of consensus as to how a trusted Bible directs prayer, planning and action in today's drifting society. We thank God for all these agreements, which we believe to be of great significance for our time.

Approaching Contemporary Problems

The process of supernatural divine action that produced the canonical Scriptures gave us, not a students' textbook of theology and ethics, but something richer and more instructive—a book of life. In this book, consisting as it does of sixty-six separate books, many different kinds of material are brought together. The backbone of the Bible is a collection of historical narratives spanning some thousands of years and telling how God the Creator became God the Redeemer after sin had entered His world and spoiled humanity. All the didactic, doctrinal, devotional, moral and liturgical material, whether in the form of sermons, letters, hymns, prayers, laws, rubrics, proverbs, philosophical and practical reflections, or any other type of writing, has the character of occasional applicatory exposition addressed to specific people, in their historical and theological location at one particular point in God's unfolding plan of revelation and redemption. Because this is so, and in light of the massive cultural distance between the ancient Near Eastern civilizations out of which the Bible came, and the community life of the modern West, seeing the truest and wisest application of biblical principles to life today is often a task of some difficulty. Universal truths about God and men in relation to each other have to be unshelled from the applications in which we find them encased when first we meet them, and reapplied in cultural contexts and within a flow of history quite different from anything exhibited by the biblical text. In applying Scripture to this changed and changing milieu of our own times, the following principles must ever be borne in mind.

First, since all Scripture is authenticated to us as the permanently authoritative Word of God by our Lord Jesus Christ Himself (our Old Testament by His attestation and use of it, our New Testament by His promise of the Spirit to its apostolic and prophetic writers), it ought to be viewed in its entirety as the organ and channel of Christ's own authority. Thus, faithful discipleship to Christ must be held to involve conscientious acceptance of all that Scripture teaches, whether in the indicative or the imperative mood, and the common idea that loyalty to Christ can consist with sceptical or selective approaches to Scripture must be dismissed as a perverse and indefensible fancy. The authority of Scripture and the authority of Christ are one.

Second, since all Scripture is ultimately the product of a single mind, that of God the Holy Spirit, there is real consistency in its teaching on every subject which it touches. Any appearance of self-contradiction or confusion should therefore be judged illusory, and it should be understood that part of the exegete's task is to seek ways of dispelling any such appearance. How far we can succeed in this in particular cases will vary, but the goal must be aimed at always. The internal harmony of Scripture is axiomatic, being entailed by the certainty that the God of truth, from whom all biblical teaching derives, always knows his own mind, and never fudges facts. So, inasmuch as it is God's nature to speak only what is true and trustworthy, all that Scripture is found to teach on any subject is to be received as reliable. (Fuller justification for this assumption of authoritative biblical inerrancy and definitive instruction from our Creator Himself was set out in the findings of the first two Summits.)

Third, the differences between the successive stages of God's revelatory program must be kept in view, and we must be alert to the fact that some of God's requirements of His people in pre-New Testament times were temporary only. In recognizing this, however, we must also seek to discern the abiding moral and spiritual principles which these requirements were applying and expressing, and we must press the question of how these same principles bear on our lives today.

Fourth, the church is neither a source of infallible information about God apart from Scripture, nor is it in any of its modes or means of self-expression an infallible interpreter of Scripture. The church is under the Bible, not over it. The historic claims of the Roman Catholic *magisterium* are neither biblically warranted nor intrinsically plausible; nor are claims by Protestant bodies to be led and taught by God's Spirit plausible when the positions taken are not supported by biblical teaching. But centuries of biblical study have shown over and over again that canonical Scripture interprets itself from within on all matters of significance for the life of faith, hope, obedience, love and salvation. The virtual unanimity on these essentials of Bible-believing expositors since the Reformation powerfully confirms the Reformers' contention that Scripture as we have it is both *sufficient* and *perspicuous*—in other words, is complete as a revelation of God and *clear* in its meaning and message to all who through the grace of the Holy Spirit have eyes to see what lies open before them. Yet, because the intellectual sanctification of Christians, like other aspects of their sanctification, is still imperfect, some differences of opinion on secondary issues are only to be expected among Bible-believers; nor should these be thought to throw doubt on the intrinsic clarity of the Scriptures that all seek to expound and apply.

Fifth, it is a mistake of method to relativize biblical teaching to the cultural axioms, assumptions and paradigms of this or any age. Scripture discloses the work, ways and will of the unchanging Creator in relation to mankind as such, and all human opinion regarding values, priorities, and duties must be judged and where necessary corrected by reference to this disclosure. Every culture, being an expression of the corporate goals of fallen mankind, has a distorting, smothering, and blunting effect on the biblical truths which, if applied, would change it, and to keep those truths in shape, free from compromising assimilation to the cultural status quo, is never easy. Mainstream Protestantism over the past two centuries provides a cautionary tale in this regard, for it has erred in a radical way by acquiring the habit of regularly relativizing biblical teaching to current secular fashion, whether rationalist, historicist, evolutionist, existentialist, Marxist, or whatever. But this is to forget how sin darkens and misdirects the human intellect in relation to all that ultimately matters, and to forget too that Scripture was given us to lighten our mental and spiritual darkness by showing us where the concepts and conceits of secular culture in this and every other age fall short. With regard to God and human living, secular culture is always astray (see Romans 1:18-32), and only the contents of the biblical revelation can bring about the needed correction. Our calling, therefore, is not to set the Bible straight, but to allow Scripture to set us straight. Only as we let Bible teaching, in its character as God's absolute truth, amend assumptions concerning God and the best way of living that society around us takes for granted, shall we handle Scripture as we should. For the right way to handle Scripture is to allow it to handle us intellectually, morally, and spiritually. This was the Reformers' point when they spoke of the necessity of Scripture: none will ever think rightly about God, nor therefore live or act as they should, without the guidance of the Bible.

The proper way to pose the hermeneutical question that is central in contemporary debate is to ask what it is in us, and in our culture, that keeps us from hearing God's unchanging Word of judgment, mercy, repentance and righteousness, as it applies to us and to our own situation. When the question is posed in this way, the door is opened to the Word of God making its proper impact on us, which otherwise it could hardly do. The form of this impact will vary from one time and place to another, for it is right that the Word should indigenize itself in every distinct culture that the human family produces; but the substance of the impact, that is, the demand for repentance and faith in Christ, worship and holiness before God, and love and justice towards our fellow-men, will be always and everywhere the same.

Sixth, application of biblical principles to life is always conditioned by the limits of our factual knowledge about the situation in which it is being made. Where there is dispute about matters of fact, or about the likely consequences, direct or indirect, of alternative lines of action, the long-term effects, for instance, of particular industrial developments, or economic procedures, or military strategies, disagreement about the best and wisest way to move ahead is likely to follow and such disagreement may well be found disturbing, since the production of the best lawful consequences for others is part of the duty of loving our neighbour which Scripture imposes on us all. But disagreement of this kind will not necessarily imply uncertainty about the principles to be applied, and may not therefore be appealed to uncritically as evidence of different understandings of the teaching of the inerrant Scriptures.

Seventh, application of biblical principles to life requires awareness that within the limits set by the moral laws of God are areas of liberty within which we have responsibility to choose the options that seem to us most fruitful for the glory of God and the welfare of humankind, ourselves included. Never to let the good become the enemy of the best, or to prefer what seems "not bad" over what is clearly better, is one of the rules of Christian wisdom and obedience. Here again, however, Christians whose theologies agree in substance may have differences due to personal or cultural factors that rightly affect their scale of values and priorities, and once more it will be a mistake to appeal to such differences as indicating disagreement on what the Bible has to say.

Eighth, application of Scripture to life requires the unction of the Holy Spirit. Without his aid the spiritual realities of which Scripture speaks will not be perceived, nor will the scope, thrust, and searching power of biblical teaching be truly grasped, nor will the range and depth of biblical visions, pleas, challenges, rebukes, and calls to faith and amendment be properly understood. Humble recognition that there is always more to be learned, and that one's present knowledge is incomplete, and constant crying to God for more light and wisdom, is the only healthy frame of mind for those who would set forth the relevance of the divine Word. And that frame of mind will only become reality in those who are savingly related to Jesus Christ, having felt the blindness and folly of their own natural reason and thus been taught by the Lord himself not to lean to their own understanding.

Summit III assumes these eight principles as common ground, and its findings reflect an honest attempt to follow their lead rationally and self-critically in bringing scriptural teaching to bear on the world around us.

New Vistas Along Old Paths

The task to which Summit III addressed itself is to apply the teaching of a trusted Bible to some of the most confused areas of modern life. This task could not in principle be tackled by Western secular society itself: for our secular society insists on judging itself, not by the revelation of the Creator that the Bible sets forth, but by evolutionary, permissive, materialistic, hedonistic, and this-worldly yardsticks for thought. The Summit's findings embody the view that the belief and value-system that such judging reflects is in fact tragically mistaken, and the findings as a whole constitute a radical challenge to it. There is no doubt, however, that in the Western world secular perspectives everywhere ride high, and it will take a great deal more than the critique and challenge of any one conference to unseat them.

Nor could the task that Summit III undertakes be discharged by any form of liberal or modernist theology. These nominally Christian infidelities also ride high at present in certain circles: But such theology calls in question the divinity, adequacy, and binding force of much biblical teaching, and is thus methodologically incapable of operating under the authority of Scripture. The assumptions of liberalism relativize the Bible by absolutizing positions that run counter to biblical teaching (e.g., the essential goodness of man, or the essential oneness of all religions), and then rearranging biblical priorities in light of present-day secular prejudices and preoccupations (e.g., redefining mission so as to give political, social, and economic causes priority over church-planting evangelism). The Summit distances itself explicitly from the arbitrariness of any such method and the wrongheadedness of any such conclusions.

The Summit findings turn their back on all forms of that modern Athenianism that seeks only to speak or hear some new thing. Instead of pursuing novelty, they offer updated applications of an older, more stable, arguably wiser and demonstrably more biblical heritage of belief. Thus to swim against the stream of current thought is a gesture, not of timidity, but of boldness, and not of eccentricity, but of conscience. The Summit members are united in the belief that the only good way for church and community today lies along the old paths. Thus, on historic questions like the sanctity of life, of sex, and of the family, and the God-given role of the state, in its regulating of political, judicial, and economic aspects of community life, as also on questions with new late-twentieth-century angles, like the legitimacy of nuclear war and the stewardship of the natural order, the continuing validity of standpoints maintained in the Christian past is constantly asserted. By the same token, modern statism, with its worship of centralization, its pervasively paternalist ethos, and its ready sanctioning of objectionable views on all the topics mentioned, is constantly viewed as a development to regret, whether in its fascist or Marxist form or in any other. Whether this is political prejudice or prophetic vision is a question to which different people will no doubt give different answers, but it is one on which the Summit members have a fairly united mind. The two hundred and fifty of us who have met at the Summit believe that anyone who allows Scripture to deliver its own message on these matters will end up approximately where we stand ourselves. We now offer our findings and papers to the public as testimony to what we believe we have heard God say, and we shall welcome every opportunity to elaborate and confirm this testimony in wider discussions.

PREFACE

This statement is the third and final in a trilogy of Summits sponsored by the International Council on Biblical Inerrancy. Summit I (October 26-28, 1978) produced the Chicago Statement on Biblical Inerrancy. Summit II (November 10-13, 1982) resulted in the Chicago Statement on Biblical Hermeneutics. This last conference, Summit III (December 10-13, 1986), drafted the Chicago Statement on Biblical Application. With this statement the proposed scholarly work of ICBI has been completed, for the doctrine of inerrancy has thus been defined, interpreted, and applied by many of the leading evangelical scholars of our day.

NOTE: The participants at Summit III signed the following Statement of Affirmations and Denials with the following preface: "As a participant in Summit III of ICBI, I subscribe to these articles as an expression of my agreement of their overall thrust."

ARTICLES OF AFFIRMATIONS AND DENIAL

Article I : The Living God

We affirm that the one true and living God is the creator and sustainer of all things.

We affirm that this God can be known through His revelation of Himself in His inerrant written Word.

We affirm that this one God exists eternally in three persons, Father, Son, and Holy Spirit, each of whom is fully God.

We affirm that this living, acting, speaking God entered into history through the Son Jesus Christ to bring salvation to the human race.

We affirm that the revealed character and will of God are the foundation of all morality.

We deny that the human language of Scripture is inadequate to inform us who God is or what He is like. We deny that the doctrine of the Trinity is a contradiction or is based upon an unacceptable ontology.

We deny that the notion of God should be accommodated to modern thought which has no place for the concepts of sin and salvation.

Article II: The Savior and His Work

We affirm that Jesus Christ is true God, begotten from the Father from all eternity, and also true man, conceived by the Holy Spirit and born of the virgin Mary.

We affirm that the indivisible union of full deity with full humanity in the one person of Jesus Christ is essential for His saving work.

We affirm that Jesus Christ, through His vicarious suffering, death, and resurrection, is the only Savior and Redeemer of the world.

We affirm that salvation is by faith alone in Jesus Christ alone.

We affirm that Jesus Christ, as revealed in Scripture, is the supreme model of the godly life that is ours in and through Him.

We deny that Scripture warrants any proclamation or offer of salvation except on the basis of the saving work of the crucified and risen Christ.

We deny that those who die without Christ can be saved in the life to come.

We deny that persons capable of rational choice can be saved without personal faith in the biblical Christ.

We deny that presenting Jesus Christ as a moral example without reference to His deity and substitutionary atonement does justice to the teaching of Scripture.

We deny that a proper understanding of the love and justice of God warrants the hope of universal salvation.

Article III : The Holy Spirit and His Work

We affirm that the Holy Spirit is the third person of the Triune Godhead and that His work is essential for the salvation of sinners.

We affirm that true and saving knowledge of God is given by the Spirit of God as He authenticates and illuminates the Word of canonical Scripture, of which He is the primary author.

We affirm that the Holy Spirit guides the people of God, giving them wisdom to apply Scripture to modern issues and everyday life.

We affirm that the church's vitality in worship and fellowship, its faithfulness in confession, its fruitfulness in witness, and its power in mission, depend directly on the power of the Holy Spirit.

We deny that any view that disputes the essential tripersonality of the one God is compatible with the gospel.

We deny that any person can say from the heart that Jesus is Lord apart from the Holy Spirit.

We deny that the Holy Spirit, since the apostolic age, has ever given, or does now give, new normative revelation to the church.

We deny that the name of renewal should be given to any movement in the church that does not involve a deepened sense of God's judgment and mercy in Christ.

Article IV: The Church and Its Mission

We affirm that the inspiration of the Holy Spirit gives the Bible its canonical authority, and the role of the church was and is to recognize and affirm this authority.

We affirm that Christ the Lord has established his church on earth and rules it by His Word and Spirit.

We affirm that the church is apostolic as it receives and is established upon the doctrine of the apostles recorded in Scripture and continues to proclaim the apostolic gospel.

We affirm that identifying marks of local churches are faithful confession and proclamation of the Word of God, and responsible administration of baptism and the Lord's Supper.

We affirm that churches are subject to the Word of Christ in their order as in their doctrine.

We affirm that in addition to their commitment to a local church, Christians may properly involve themselves in parachurch organizations for specialized ministry.

We affirm that Christ calls the church to serve Him by its worship, nurture, and witness as His people in the world.

We affirm that Christ sends the church into the whole world to summon sinful humanity to faith, repentance, and righteousness.

We affirm that the unity and clarity of Scripture encourage us to seek to resolve doctrinal differences among Christians, and so to manifest the oneness of the church in Christ.

We deny that the church can grant canonical authority to Scripture.

We deny that the church is constituted by the will and traditions of men.

We deny that the church can bind the conscience apart from the Word of God.

We deny that the church can free itself from the authority of the written Word of God and still exercise valid discipline in Christ's name.

We deny that the church can accommodate itself to the demands of a particular culture if those demands conflict with scriptural revelation, or if they restrain the liberty of Christian conscience.

We deny that differing cultural situations invalidate the biblical principle of male-female equality or the biblical requirements for their roles in the church.

Article V : Sanctity of Human Life

We affirm that God the Creator is sovereign over all human life and mankind is responsible under God to preserve and protect it.

We affirm that the sanctity of human life is based on the creation of mankind in the image and likeness of God.

We affirm that the life of a human being begins at conception (fertilization) and continues until biological death; thus, abortion (except where the continuance of the pregnancy imminently threatens the mother's physical life), infanticide, suicide, and euthanasia are forms of murder.

We affirm that the penal view of social justice is compatible with the sanctity of human life.

We affirm that withholding food or water in order to cause or hasten death is a violation of the sanctity of life.

We affirm that because advancing medical technology has obscured the distinction between life and death, it is essential to evaluate each terminal case with the greatest care so as to preserve the sanctity of human life.

We deny that the quality of human life has priority over its sanctity.

We deny that the sanctity of pre-natal life negates the propriety of necessary medical procedures to preserve the life of the pregnant mother.

We deny that killing in self-defense, in state-administered capital punishment, or in wars justly fought, is necessarily a violation of the sanctity of human life.

We deny that those who reject a divine basis for moral law are exempt from the ethical and social obligation to preserve and protect innocent human life.

We deny that allowing death without medical intervention to prolong life is always a violation of the sanctity of human life.

Article VI: Marriage and the Family

We affirm that the purpose of marriage is to glorify God and extend His Kingdom on earth in an institution that provides for chastity, companionship, procreation and Christian upbringing of children.

We affirm that since marriage is a sacred covenant under God uniting a man and a woman as one flesh, church and state should require faithfulness to God's intention that it be a permanent bond.

We affirm that in the marriage pattern ordained by God, the husband as head is the loving servant-leader of his wife, and the wife as helper in submissive companionship is a full partner with her husband.

We affirm that loving nurture and discipline of children is a God-ordained duty of parents, and God-ordained obedience to parents is a duty of children.

We affirm that the church has the responsibility to nurture the family.

We affirm that honor to parents is a life-long duty of all persons and includes responsibility for the care of the aged.

We affirm that the family should perform many services now commonly assumed by the state.

We deny that pleasure and self-fulfillment are the basis of marriage and that hardships are justifiable cause for breaking the marriage covenant.

We deny that the biblical ideal of marriage can be fulfilled either by a couple living together without a lawful marriage covenant or by any form of same-sex or group cohabitation.

We deny that the state has the right to legitimize views of marriage and the family unit that contravene biblical standards.

We deny that changing social conditions ever make God-ordained marriage or family roles obsolete or irrelevant.

We deny that the state has the right to usurp biblically designated parental responsibility.

Article VII: Divorce and Remarriage

We affirm that the marriage of Adam and Eve as a lifelong monogamous relationship is the pattern for all marriages within the human race.

We affirm that God unites husband and wife in every covenanted and consummated marriage, and will hold covenant-breakers morally accountable.

We affirm that since the essence of the marriage covenant is life-long commitment to the covenant partner, action in relation to a marital breakdown should at least initially aim at the reconciliation of the partners and restoration of the marriage.

We affirm that God hates divorce, however motivated.

We affirm that although God hates divorce, in a sinful world separation is sometimes advisable and divorce is sometimes inevitable.

We affirm that God forgives repentant sinners, even those who have sinned by sundering their marriages.

We affirm that the local church has the responsibility to discipline those who violate the biblical standards for marriage, compassionately restore those who repent, and faithfully minister God's grace to those whose lives have been scarred by marital disruption.

We deny that any contradiction exists within Scripture on the subject of divorce and remarriage.

We deny that it is sinful to separate or live apart from a promiscuous or abusive spouse.

Article VIII: Sexual Deviations

We affirm that Scripture reveals God's standards for sexual relationships, deviation from which is sinful.

We affirm that sexual intercourse is legitimate only in a heterosexual marriage relationship.

We affirm that God's grace in Christ can deliver men and women from bondage to deviant sexual practice, be they heterosexual or homosexual, and the church must assume responsibility for restoring such members to a life that honors God.

We affirm that God loves homosexuals as well as other sinners, and that homosexual temptations can be resisted in the power of Christ to the glory of His grace, just as other temptations can.

We affirm that Christians must exercise a compassion, kindness, and forgiveness in the ministry of God's grace to those whose lives have been scarred by sexual deviations.

We affirm that human fulfillment does not depend on satisfying sexual drives; hedonism and related philosophies encouraging promiscuous sexuality are wrong and lead to ruin.

We affirm that pornography threatens the well-being of individuals, families, and entire societies, and that it is incumbent upon Christians to seek to check its production and distribution.

We deny that homosexual practice can ever please God.

We deny that heredity, childhood conditioning, or other environmental influences can excuse deviant sexual behavior.

We deny that the sexual molestation or exploitation of children in general and incestuous relationships in particular can ever be justified.

We deny that it is hopeless to look for deliverance from homosexual practices or other forms of sexual deviancy.

We deny that the healing of sexual deviancy is aided by condemnation without compassion or by compassion without the application of Scriptural truth, in confident hope.

Article IX: The State Under God

We affirm that God established civil government as an instrument of His common grace, to restrain sin, to maintain order, and to promote civil justice and general well-being.

We affirm that God gives civil governments the right to use coercive force for the defense and encouragement of those who do good and for the just punishment of those who do evil.

We affirm that it is proper and desirable that Christians take part in civil government and advocate the enactment of laws for the common good in accordance with God's moral law.

We affirm that it is the duty of Christian people to pray for civil authorities and to obey them, except when such obedience would involve the violation of God's moral law or neglect the God-ordained responsibilities of Christian witness.

We affirm that governments have a responsibility before God to establish and enforce laws that accord with God's moral law as it pertains to human relations.

We affirm that Christ's rule of the church through His Word must not be confused with the power He grants to civil governments; such confusion will compromise the purity of the gospel and will violate the conscience of individuals.

We affirm that when families or churches neglect their biblically defined duties, thus jeopardizing the wellbeing of their members, the state may rightfully intervene.

We deny that the state has the right to usurp authority of other God-given spheres of life, especially in the church and in the family.

We deny that the Kingdom of God can be established by the coercive power of civil governments.

We deny that the state has the right to forbid voluntary prayer and other voluntary religious exercises at an appropriate time in the public school.

We deny that God's providential establishment of a particular government confers special blessing, apart from the government's just and faithful execution of its duties.

We deny that religious belief is an essential prerequisite to service in civil government, or that its absence invalidates the legal authority of those who govern.

We deny the Kingdom of God can be established by the power of civil governments.

We deny that the government has the right to prescribe specific prayers or forms of religious exercise for its citizens.

Article X: Law and Justice

We affirm that the Scriptures are the only infallible record of unchanging moral principles basic to a sound jurisprudence and an adequate philosophy of human rights.

We affirm that God has impressed His image on the hearts of all people so that they are morally accountable to Him for their actions as individuals and as members of society.

We affirm that God's revealed law, the moral nature of mankind, and human legislation serve to restrain the fallen political order from chaos and anarchy and to point humankind to the need for redemption in Jesus Christ.

We affirm that the Gospel cannot be legislated and the Law cannot save sinners.

We deny that legal positivism, or any other humanistic philosophy of law, is able to satisfy the need for absolute standards of law and justice.

We deny that any person or any society fulfills God's standards so as to justify himself, herself, or itself before the tribunal of God's absolute justice.

We deny that any political, economic, or social order is free from the deadly consequences of original sin or capable of offering a utopian solution or substitute for the perfect society which Christ alone will establish at His Second Coming.

Article XI: War

We affirm that God desires peace and righteousness among nations and condemns wars of aggression.

We affirm that lawful states have the right and duty to defend their territories and citizens against aggression and oppression by other powers, including the provision for an adequate civil defense of the population.

We affirm that in rightful defense of their territories and citizens' governments should only use just means of warfare.

We affirm that warring states should strive by every means possible to minimize civilian casualties.

We deny that the cause of Christ can be defended with earthly weapons.

We deny that Christians are forbidden to use weapons in the defense of lawful states.

We deny that the indiscriminate slaughter of civilians can be a moral form of warfare.

We deny that the circumstances of modern warfare destroy the right and duty of the civil government to defend its territories and citizens.

Article XII: Discrimination and Human Rights

We affirm that God, who created man and woman in His image, has granted to all human beings fundamental rights which are to be protected, sustained, and fostered on the natural and spiritual levels.

We affirm that all human beings are ultimately accountable to God for their use of these rights.

We affirm that Christians must uphold and defend the rights of others while being willing to relinquish their own rights for the good of others.

We affirm that Christians are admonished to follow the compassionate example of Jesus by helping to bear the burdens of those whose human rights have been diminished.

We deny that any so-called human right which violates the teaching of Scripture is legitimate.

We deny that any act is acceptable that would harm or diminish another person's natural or spiritual life by violating that person's human rights.

We deny that age, disability, economic disadvantage, race, religion, or sex used as a basis for discrimination can ever justify denial of the exercise or enjoyment of human rights.

We deny that elitism or grasping for power are compatible with Christ's call to dedicate our rights to His service.

Article XIII: Economics

We affirm that valid economic principles can be found in Scripture and should form an integral part of a Christian world and life view.

We affirm that material resources are a blessing from God, to be enjoyed with thanksgiving, and are to be earned, managed, and shared as a stewardship under God.

We affirm that Christians should give sacrificially of their resources to support the work of God's church.

We affirm that the use of personal and material resources for the proclamation of the gospel is necessary both for the salvation of lost mankind and to overcome poverty where that is fostered by adherence to non-Christian religious systems.

We affirm that active compassion for the poor and oppressed is an obligation that God places upon all human beings, especially on those with resources.

We affirm that the possession of wealth imposes obligations upon its possessors.

We affirm that the love of money is a source of great evil.

We affirm that human depravity, greed, and the will to power foster economic injustice and subvert concern for the poor.

We affirm that the Bible affirms the right of private ownership as a stewardship under God.

We deny that Scripture directly teaches any science of economics, although there are principles of economics that can be derived from Scripture.

We deny that Scripture teaches that compassion for the poor must be expressed exclusively through one particular economic system.

We deny that the Scripture teaches that money or wealth is inherently evil.

We deny that Scripture endorses economic collectivism or economic individualism.

We deny that Scripture forbids the use of capital resources to produce income.

We deny that the proper focus of a Christian's hope is material prosperity.

We deny that Christians should use their resources primarily for self-gratification.

We deny that salvation from sin necessarily involves economic or political liberation.

Article XIV: Work and Leisure

We affirm that God created humankind in His image and graciously fitted them for both work and leisure.

We affirm that in all honorable work, however menial, God works with and through the worker.

We affirm that work is the divinely ordained means whereby we glorify God and supply both our own needs and the needs of others.

We affirm that Christians should work to the best of their ability so as to please God.

We affirm that people should both humbly submit to and righteously exercise whatever authority operates in their sphere of work.

We affirm that in their work people should seek first God's kingdom and righteousness, depending on Him to supply their material needs.

We affirm that compensation should be a fair return for the work done without discrimination.

We affirm that leisure, in proper balance with work, is ordained by God and should be enjoyed to His glory.

We affirm that work and its product have not only temporal but also eternal value when done and used for God's glory.

We deny that persons should pursue their work to fulfill and gratify themselves rather than to serve and please God.

We deny that the rich have more right to leisure than the poor.

We deny that certain types of work give persons greater value in God's eyes than other persons have.

We deny that the Christian should either depreciate leisure or make a goal of it.

Article XV: Wealth and Poverty

We affirm that God, who is just and loving, has a special concern for the poor in their plight,

We affirm that God calls for responsible stewardship by His people of both their lives and resources.

We affirm that sacrificial effort to relieve the poverty, oppression, and suffering of others is a hallmark of Christian discipleship.

We affirm that just as the wealthy ought not be greedy so the poor ought not to be covetous.

We deny that we may rightly call ourselves disciples of Christ if we lack active concern for the poor, oppressed, and suffering, especially those of the household of faith.

We deny that we may always regard prosperity or poverty as the measure of our faithfulness to Christ.

We deny that it is necessarily wrong for Christians to be wealthy or for some persons to possess more than others.

Article XVI: Stewardship of the Environment

We affirm that God created the physical environment for His own glory and for the good of His human creatures.

We affirm that God deputized humanity to govern the creation.

We affirm that mankind has more value than the rest of creation.

We affirm that mankind's dominion over the earth imposes a responsibility to protect and tend its life and resources.

We affirm that Christians should embrace responsible scientific investigation and its application in technology.

We affirm that stewardship of the Lord's earth includes the productive use of its resources which must always be replenished as far as possible.

We affirm that avoidable pollution of the earth, air, water, or space is irresponsible.

We deny that the cosmos is valueless apart from mankind.

We deny that the biblical view authorizes or encourages wasteful exploitation of nature.

We deny that Christians should embrace the countercultural repudiation of science or the mistaken belief that science is the hope of mankind.

We deny that individuals or societies should exploit the universe's resources for their own advantage at the expense of other people and societies.

We deny that a materialistic world view can provide an adequate basis for recognizing environmental values.

BOOK IV

EXPLAINING INERRANCY

A COMMENTARY ON THE CHICAGO STATEMENT

Robert Charles Sproul

This book was first published in 1980 by the ICBI as an official ICBI sanctioned publication under the title *Explaining Inerrancy: A Commentary*. It was republished with the title *Explaining Inerrancy* in 1996 and retitled *Can I Trust the Bible?* in 2009 by Reformation Trust, a division of Ligonier Ministries. It is reproduced here with the permission of both Ligonier Ministries and R.C. Sproul.

Copyright © 1996 Ligonier Ministries
All rights reserved.

FOREWORD

The International Council on Biblical Inerrancy is a California-based organization founded in 1977. It has as its purpose the defense and application of the doctrine of biblical inerrancy as an essential element for the authority of Scripture and a necessity for the health of the church. It was created to counter the drift from this important doctrinal foundation by significant segments of evangelicalism and the outright denial of it by other church movements.

On October 26-28, 1978, the International Council on Biblical Inerrancy held a summit meeting near the Chicago airport. At that time it issued a statement on biblical inerrancy which included a Preamble, a Short Statement, Nineteen Articles of Affirmation and Denial and a more ample Exposition. Materials to be submitted to the meeting had been prepared by Drs. Edmond P. Clowney, J.I. Packer and R. C. Sproul. These were discussed in a number of ways by groups of delegates from the Advisory Board and by various partial and plenary sessions at the summit. Furthermore, written comments were solicited and received in considerable numbers. A Draft Committee composed of Drs. Edmund P. Clowney, Norman L. Geisler, Harold W. Hoehner, Donald E. Hoke, Roger R. Nicole, James

I. Packer, Earl D. Radmacher, and R. C. Sproul labored very hard and literally around the clock to prepare a statement that might receive the approval of a great majority of the participants. Very special attention was devoted to the Nineteen Articles of Affirmation and Denial. (The preamble and the short statement were also subjected to editorial revisions. The exposition was left largely as received.) After considerable discussion what was submitted received a very substantial endorsement by the participants: 240 (out of a total of 268) actually affixed their signatures to the Nineteen Articles.

It was indicated that the Draft Committee would meet within the year to review and, if necessary, revise the statement. Their meeting took place in the fall of 1979 with Drs. Norman L. Geisler, Harold W. Hoehner, Roger R. Nicole and Earl D. Radmacher in attendance. It was the consensus of those present that we should not undertake to modify a statement that so many people had signed, both at the summit meeting and afterwards. But in order to ward off misunderstandings, and to provide an exposition of the position advocated by the ICBI, it was thought desirable to provide a commentary on each of the Articles. A draft was prepared to this effect by Dr. R. C. Sproul, and this was submitted to the members of the Draft Committee. A number of editorial changes were made, and it is this which is now offered to the public.

Dr. Sproul is well qualified to write such a commentary. He had prepared the first draft of the Nineteen Articles, and although this underwent considerable change in the editing process, Dr. Sproul was closely related to all discussions conducted by the Draft Committee. The present, more extensive text will make clear even to those who are not fully abreast of current discussions on inspiration exactly what is meant to be affirmed and denied. Obviously, those who have signed the Articles will not necessarily concur in every interpretation advocated by the commentary. Not even the members of the Draft Committee are bound by this, and perhaps not even Dr. Sproul, since his text underwent certain editorial revisions. However, this commentary does represent an effort at making clear the precise position of the International Council on Biblical Inerrancy as a whole.

In the editing process we strove to take account of the comments that were forwarded to us. In some cases we could not concur with those who made comments, and therefore the changes solicited could not be made. In other cases, matters were brought to our notice which in our judgment deserved consideration. We trust that the commentary will remove ambiguities and deal effectively with possible misunderstandings.

There is a remarkable unity of views among the members of the Council and the Board, and this should be reflected not only in the Articles in their original form but also in the present pamphlet. It has not been the aim of those who were gathered at Chicago to break relations with those who do not share our convictions concerning the doctrine of Scripture. Rather, the aim has been and continues to be to bear witness to what we are convinced is the biblical doctrine on the great subject of the inspiration of Scripture. We hope in making this confession and presenting this commentary to dispel misunderstandings with which the doctrine of inerrancy has so frequently been burdened and to present with winsomeness and clarity this great tenet in witness to which we are gladly uniting.

Roger R. Nicole

COMMENTARY

R.C. SPROUL

The Word of God and Authority

The Chicago Statement on Biblical Inerrancy, adopted at a meeting of more than two hundred evangelical leaders in October 1978, rightly affirms that "the authority of Scripture is a key issue for the Christian church in this and every age." But authority cannot stand in isolation, as the Statement shows. The authority of the Bible is based on its being the written Word of God, and because the Bible is the Word of God and the God of the Bible is Truth and speaks truthfully, authority is linked to inerrancy. If the Bible is the Word of God and if God is a God of truth, then the Bible must be inerrant—not merely in some of its parts, as some modern theologians are saying, but totally, as the church for the most part has said down through the ages of its history.

Some of the terms used in the debate about the authority and inerrancy of the Bible are technical ones. Some show up in the Chicago Statement, but they are not difficult to come to understand. They can be mastered (and the doctrine of inerrancy more fully understood) by a little reading and study. This commentary on the

Chicago Statement attempts to provide such material in reference to the Nineteen Articles of Affirmation and Denial, which form the heart of the document. The full text of the Statement appears as an Appendix.

ARTICLE I
Authority

We affirm that the Holy Scriptures are to be received as the authoritative Word of God.

We deny that the Scriptures receive their authority from the church, tradition or any other human source.

The initial article of the Chicago Statement is designed to establish the degree of authority that is to be attributed to the Bible. This article, as well as Article II, makes the statement clearly a Protestant one. Though it is true that the Roman Catholic Church has consistently and historically maintained a high view of the inspiration of Holy Scripture, there remains the unresolved problem of the uniqueness and sufficiency of biblical authority for the church.

Rome has placed alongside of Scripture the traditions of the church as a supplement to Scripture and, consequently, a second source of special revelation beyond the scope of Scripture. It has been a continuous assertion of the Roman Catholic Church that since the church established the extent and scope of the New Testament and Old Testament canon there is a certain sense in which the authority of the Bible is subordinate to and dependent upon the church's approval. It is particularly these issues of the relationship of church and canon and of the question of multiple sources of special revelation that are in view with both Article I and Article II.

In earlier drafts of Article I the extent of this canon was spelled out to include the 66 canonical books that are found and embraced within the context of most Protestant-sanctioned editions of the Bible. In discussions among the participants of the Summit and because of requests to the drafting committee, there was considerable sentiment for striking the words "66 canonical books" from the earlier drafts. This was due to some variance within Christendom as to the exact number of books that are to be recognized within the canon. For example, the Ethiopic Church has more books included in their canon than 66. The final draft affirms simply that the *Holy Scriptures* are to be received as the authoritative Word of God. For the vast majority of Protestants the designation "Holy Scripture" has clear reference to the 66 canonical books, but it leaves room for those who differ on the canon question to participate in the confession of the nature of Scripture. The specific question of the number of books contained in that canon is left open in this Statement.

The whole question of the scope of canon or the list of books that make up our Bible may be one that confuses many people, particularly those who are accustomed to a clearly defined number of books by their particular church confessions. Some have argued that if one questions a particular book's canonicity this carries with it the implication that one does not believe in a divinely inspired Bible. Perhaps the clearest illustration of this in history is the fact that Martin Luther at one point in his ministry had strong reservations about including the book of James in the New Testament canon. Though it is abundantly clear that Luther believed in an inspired Bible, he still had questions about whether or not a particular book should be included in that inspired Bible. Several scholars have tried to deny that Luther ever believed in inspiration because of his questioning of the book of James. Here it is very important to see the difference between the question of the scope of the canon and the question of the inspiration of the books which are recognized as included in the canon. In other words, the nature of Scripture and the question of the extent of Scripture are two different questions which must not be confused.

A key word in the affirmation section of Article I is the word "received." The initial draft mentioned that the Scriptures are to be received by the church. The phrase "by the church" has been deleted because it is clear that the Word of God in Holy Scripture is to be received not only by the church, but by everyone. The word "received" has historical significance. In the church councils that considered the canon question the Latin word *recipimus* was used, meaning "we receive" the following books to be included in the canon. In that usage of the word "receive," it is clear that the church was not declaring certain books to be authoritative by virtue of the church's prior authority, but that the church was simply acknowledging the Word of God to be the Word of God. By the word "receive" they displayed their willingness to submit to what they regarded to be already the Word of God. Consequently, any notion that the church creates the Bible or is superior to the Bible is eliminated.

If any ambiguity about the relationship of Scripture to the church remains in the affirmation, it is removed in the subsequent denial: the Scriptures receive their authority from God, not from the church nor from any other human source.

ARTICLE II
Scripture and Tradition

> *We affirm that the Scriptures are the supreme written norm by which God binds the conscience, and that the authority of the church is subordinate to that of Scripture.*
>
> *We deny that church creeds, councils or declarations have authority greater than or equal to the authority of the Bible.*

Article II of the Chicago Statement reinforces Article I and goes into more detail concerning the matters involved with it. Article II has in view the classical Protestant principle of *sola scriptura* which speaks of the unique authority of the Bible with respect to binding the consciences of men. The affirmation of Article II speaks of the Scriptures as "the supreme written norm." Discussion concerning the word "supreme" was lengthy; alternate words were suggested and subsequently eliminated from the text. Words like "ultimate" and "only" were discarded in favor of "supreme." The question at this point dealt with the fact that other written documents are important to the life of the church. For example, church creeds and confessions form the basis of subscription and unity of faith in many different Christian denominations and communities. Such creeds and confessions have a kind of normative authority within a given Christian body and have the effect of binding consciences within that particular context. However, it is a classic tenet of Protestants to recognize that all such creeds and confessions are fallible and cannot fully and finally bind the conscience of an individual believer. Only the Word of God has the kind of authority that can bind the conscience of men forever. So, though the articles acknowledge that there are other written norms recognized by different bodies of Christians, insofar as they are true, those written norms are derived from and are subordinate to the supreme written norm which is the Holy Scripture.

In the denial it is clearly spelled out that no church creed, council or declaration has authority greater than or equal to the authority of the Bible. Again, any idea of an equal authority level of tradition or church officers is repudiated by this statement. The whole question of a Christian's obedience to authority structures apart from the Scripture was a matter of great discussion with regard to this article. For example, the Bible itself exhorts us to obey the civil magistrates. We are certainly willing to subject ourselves to our own church confessions and to the authority structure of our ecclesiastical bodies. But the thrust of this article is to indicate that whatever lesser authorities there are, they never carry with them the authority of God Himself. There is a sense in which all authority in this world is derived and dependent upon the authority of God. God and God alone has intrinsic authority. That intrinsic authority is the authority given to the Bible since it is God's Word. Various Christian bodies have defined the extent of civil authority and ecclesiastical authority in different ways. For example, in Reformed churches the authority of the church is viewed as ministerial and declarative rather than ultimate and intrinsic. God and God alone has the absolute right to bind the consciences of men. Our consciences are justly bound to lesser authorities only when and if they are in conformity to the Word of God.

The Word of God and Revelation

The next three articles deal with revelation. Article III defines what we mean when we say that the Bible is revelation and not merely a witness to revelation, as is affirmed by the neo-orthodox theologians. Article IV considers the use of human language as a vehicle for divine revelation. Article V notes the way in which the revelation of God unfolds progressively throughout Scripture so that later texts more fully expound the earlier ones. In these articles the framers of the Statement guard against any view which would lessen the unique nature of the Bible as God's written revelation or negate the teaching of some parts of it by appeal to other parts.

ARTICLE III
Revelation

We affirm that the written Word in its entirety is revelation given by God.

We deny that the Bible is merely a witness to revelation, or only becomes revelation in encounter, or depends on the responses of men for its validity.

Both the affirmation and denial of Article III have in view the controversial question of the objective character of divine revelation in Scripture. There has been considerable debate in the twentieth century on this issue, particularly with the rise of so-called dialectical or "Neo-Orthodox" theology. This approach sought to promote a "dynamic" view of Scripture which sees the authority of Scripture functioning in a dynamic relationship of Word and hearing of the Word. Several theologians have denied that the Bible in and of itself, objectively, is revelation. They maintain that revelation does not occur until or unless there is an inward, subjective human response to that Word. Scholars like Emil Brunner, for example, have insisted that the Bible is not itself revelation, but is merely a witness to that revelation which is found in Christ. It has been fashionable in certain quarters to maintain that special revelation is embodied in Christ and in Christ alone, and that to consider the Bible as objective revelation would be to detract from the uniqueness of the person of Jesus Christ who is the Word made flesh.

The spirit of these articles is to oppose a disjunction between the revelation that is given to us in the person of Christ objectively and the revelation that comes to us in equally objective terms in the Word of God inscripturated. Here the Bible is seen not merely as a catalyst for revelation, but as revelation itself. If the Bible is God's Word and its content proceeds from Him, then its content is to be seen as revelation. Here revelation is viewed as "propositional." It is propositional not because the Bible is written in the style of logical equations or analytical formulas. It is propositional because it communicates a content which may be understood as propositions.

In the affirmation of Article III the words "in its entirety" are also significant. There are those who have claimed that the Bible contains here and there, in specified places, revelation from God, but that it is the task of the believer individually or the church corporately to separate the parts of Scripture which are revelatory from those which are not. This article by implication repudiates such an approach to Scripture inasmuch as the whole of Scripture, its entire contents, is to be seen as being divine revelation.

The denial stated in Article III reinforces the objectivity of revelation in Scripture and maintains that the validity of that revelation does not depend upon human responses. The Bible's truth does not depend in any way on whether or not a person believes the truth.

The central thrust of Article III is to declare with confidence that the content of Scripture is not the result of human imagination or cleverly devised philosophical opinions, but that it reflects God's sovereign disclosure about himself and all matters which are touched upon by Scripture. The Bible, then, embodies truth that comes to us from beyond the scope of our own abilities. It comes from God himself.

ARTICLE IV
Human Language

We affirm that God who made mankind in his image has used language as a means of revelation.

We deny that human language is so limited by our creatureliness that it is rendered inadequate as a vehicle for divine revelation. *We further deny* that the corruption of human culture and language through sin has thwarted God's work of inspiration.

One of the most significant attacks on biblical inerrancy that has come to light in the twentieth century is that based on the limitations of human language. Since the Bible was not written by God himself, but by human writers, the question has emerged again and again whether such human involvement by virtue of the limitations built in human creatureliness would, of necessity, render the Bible less than infallible. Since men are not infallible in and of themselves, and are prone to error in all that they do, would it not follow logically that anything coming from the pen of man must be errant? To this we reply, erroneousness is not an inevitable concomitant of human nature. Adam, before the fall, may well have been free from proneness to error, and Christ, though fully human, never erred. Since the fall it is a common tendency of men to err. We deny, however, that it is necessary for men to err always and everywhere in what they say or write, even apart from inspiration.

However, with the aid of divine inspiration and the superintendence of the Holy Spirit in the giving of sacred Scripture, the writings of the

Bible are free from the normal tendencies and propensities of fallen men to distort the truth. Though our language, and especially our language about God, is never comprehensive and exhaustive in its ability to capture eternal truths, nevertheless it is adequate to give us truth without falsehood. For example, if we made a statement that Chicago is a city in the state of Illinois, the truth communicated by that statement would in no way be exhaustive. That is, all that could possibly be understood of the nature and scope of the city of Chicago would not be known by any human being who made such a statement, nor would all the complexities that go into and comprise the state of Illinois be understood totally by the speaker. Certainly if God made the statement, "Chicago is a city in the state of Illinois," within his mind there would be total comprehension of all that is involved in Chicago and Illinois. Nevertheless, the fact that God makes the statement "Chicago is a city in the state of Illinois" would not in itself make the statement more or less true than if a human being made the statement. Though we recognize that human language is limited by creatureliness, we do not allow the inference that therefore human language must necessarily be distortive of truth.

If human language were to be judged intrinsically inadequate to convey revelation, there would be no possible means by which God could reveal anything about himself to us in verbal form. Since, however, the Bible teaches that man is created in the image of God and that there is some point of likeness between man and God, communication between God and man is possible. Such possibility of communication is built into creation by God himself.

With respect to the denial that human language is so limited that it is rendered inadequate, particularly in view of the effects of sin on our human culture and language, we must say that though man's fall renders us guilty before the divine judgment and, though "all men are liars," it does not follow necessarily that therefore "all men lie all the time." Though all of us lie at one time or another, this does not mean that we lie every time we speak. Again, that tendency toward corruption, distortion and falsehood is precisely that which we believe to be overcome by the divine inspiration and involvement in the preparation of Holy Scripture. Thus, we think that skepticism about biblical integrity based on inferences drawn from the adequacy or inadequacy of human speech is unwarranted.

ARTICLE V
Progressive Revelation

We affirm that God's revelation in the Holy Scriptures was progressive.

We deny that later revelation, which may fulfill earlier revelation, ever corrects or contradicts it. **We further deny** *that any normative revelation has been given since the completion of the New Testament writings.*

The issues in view in Article V are of profound importance to the life of the church and are very complicated at times. What is simply stated in the affirmation is a recognition that within the Bible itself there is a progressive revelation. All that has been revealed of God in the totality of Scripture is not found, for example, in the book of Genesis. Much of the content of God's redemptive activity in Christ is hinted at in part and given in shadowy ways in the earlier portions of the Old Testament. But throughout sacred Scripture the content of divine revelation is expanded, ultimately to the fullness reached in the New Testament. That is what is meant by progressive revelation in this context, that the revelation within Scripture unfolds in an ever-deepening and broadening way.

Having made that recognition, the article of denial makes clear that such progress and expansion of revelation does not deny or contradict what has been given earlier. Though certain precepts which were obligatory to people in the Old Testament period are no longer so in the New Testament, this does not mean that they were discontinued because they were wicked in the past and now God has corrected what he formerly endorsed, but rather that certain practices have become superseded by newer practices that are consistent with fulfillment of Old Testament activities. This in no way suggests that the Old Testament is irrelevant to the New Testament believer or that earlier revelation may be dismissed out of hand in light of newer revelation. The Bible is still to be regarded as a holistic book where the Old Testament helps us understand the New Testament and the New Testament sheds significant light on the Old Testament. Although progressive revelation is recognized, this progressiveness is not to be viewed as a license to play loosely with portions of Scripture, setting one dimension of revelation against another within the Bible itself. The Bible's coherency and consistency is not, vitiated by progressive revelation within it.

It is also added by way of denial that no normative revelation has been given to the church since the close of the New Testament canon. The denial does not mean that God the Holy Spirit has stopped working, or that the Holy Spirit in no way leads his people today. Part of the difficulty is that theological words are used in different ways within different Christian communities. For example, what one group may call "revelation" another group may define as "illumination." Thus the qualifying word "normative" is important to understanding the last part of the denial. What is meant here is that no revelation has been given since the first century that merits or warrants inclusion in the canon of Holy Scripture. Private leadings or guidance or "revelations," as some may term them, may not be seen as having the force or authority of Holy Scripture.

The Word of God and Inspiration

Inspiration is the way in which God gave his Word to us through human authors, but how he did is a matter not fully understood. In this section of the Articles of Affirmation and Denial the framers of the document explicitly deny understanding the mode of inspiration. But they affirm, as Scripture itself also does (2 Tim. 3:16), that the Bible is the product of divine inspiration and that this work extended through the human writers to each section and even each word of the original documents. The process of inspiration did not make the biblical writers automatons, for their books reveal differences of vocabulary, style and other matters of variation between one human author and another. But inspiration did overcome any tendency they may have had to error, with the result that the words they wrote were precisely what God, the divine author, intended us to have.

ARTICLE VI
Verbal Plenary Inspiration

We affirm that the whole of Scripture and all its parts, down to the very words of the original, were given by divine inspiration.

We deny that the inspiration of Scripture can rightly be affirmed of the whole without the parts, or of some parts but not the whole.

What is in view in Article VI is the doctrine of verbal plenary inspiration. Plenary inspiration means that the whole of Scripture is given by divine inspiration. Because some have maintained that the whole has been given by inspiration but some parts of that whole are not of divine inspiration we are speaking of the origin of Scripture, which does not begin with the insights of men, but comes from God himself.

In the affirmative section of Article VI we read the phrase "down to the very words of the original." The clause "down to the very words" refers to the extent of inspiration, and the words "of the original" indicate that it is the autographs that were inspired. The limiting of inspiration to the autographs is covered more fully later in Article X, though it is plain in this article that the verbal inspiration of the Bible refers to the original manuscripts.

The fact that Article VI speaks of divine inspiration down to the very words of the original may conjure up in some people's minds a notion of dictation of the words of Scripture by God. The doctrine of verbal plenary inspiration has often been charged with carrying with it the implication of a dictation theory of inspiration. No such theory is spelled out in this article, nor is it implied. In fact, in Article VII the framers of the statement deny the dictation theory.

The issue of dictation has raised problems in church history. In the Council of Trent in the sixteenth century the Roman Catholic Church did use the word *dictante*, meaning "dictating," with respect to the Spirit's work in the giving of the ancient texts. In the Protestant camp, John Calvin spoke of the biblical writers as being *amanuenses* or secretaries. Added to this is the complex fact that there are portions of Scripture which seem to be given by some form of dictation, such as the Ten Commandments given by God to Moses. However, in the modern era dictation as a method carries with it the canceling out of human literary styles, vocabulary choices, and the like. This article does not mean to imply such a view of inspiration that would negate or vitiate the literary styles of the individual authors of the biblical documents. The sense in which Calvin, for example, spoke of secretaries and even in which Trent spoke of dictating could hardly be construed to conform to modern methods of dictating using sophisticated equipment such as dictaphones and secretarial transcriptions. The historical context in which these words have been used in the past has specific reference to the fact that inspiration shows some analogy to a man issuing a message that is put together by a secretary. The analogy points to the question of origin of the message. In the doctrine of inspiration what is at stake is the origin of the message from God rather than from human initiation.

The mode of inspiration is left as a mystery by these articles (cf Article VII). Inspiration, as used here, involves a divine superintendence which preserved the writers in their word choices from using words that would falsify or distort the message of Scripture. Thus, on the one hand, the Statement affirms that God's superintendence and inspiration of the Bible applied down to the very words and, on the other hand, denies that he canceled out the exercise of the writers' personalities in the choices of words used to express the truth revealed.

Evangelical Christians have wanted to avoid the notion that biblical writers were passive instruments like pens in the hands of God, yet at the same time they affirm that the net result of the process of inspiration would be the same. Calvin, for example, says that we should treat the Bible as if we have heard God audibly speaking its message. That is, it carries the same weight of authority as if God himself were heard to be giving utterance to the words of Scripture. (*Institutes*, I, vii, 1; Sermons on Gospel Harmony XLVI, p. 164 and *passim*). That does not mean that Calvin believed or taught that God did in fact utter the words audibly. We do not know the process by which inspired Scripture was given. But we are saying that inspiration, however God brought it about, results in the net effect that every word of Scripture carries with it the weight of God's authority.

ARTICLE VII
Inspiration

We affirm that inspiration was the work in which God by His Spirit, through human writers, gave us His Word. The origin of Scripture is divine. The mode of divine inspiration remains largely a mystery to us.

We deny that inspiration can be reduced to human insight, or to heightened states of consciousness of any kind.

Article VII spells out in more detail what is implied in Article VI. Here clear reference is given to the human writers of the text. The human writers become the human instruments by which God's Word comes to us. Classically the Holy Scriptures have been called the *Verbum Dei*, the Word of God, or even the *vox Dei*, the voice of God. Yet, at the same time, Holy Scripture comes to us as the words of men. In other words, there is an agency of humanity through which

God's divine Word is communicated; yet the origin of Scripture is divine.

What the framers of the document have in view here is the primary meaning of the word *theopneustos* in 2 Timothy 3:16, the word translated "inspired by God." The word *theopneustos* means literally "God breathed" and has primary reference to God's breathing out his word rather than breathing in some kind of effect upon human writers. So expiration is a more accurate term than inspiration with respect to the origin of Scripture. But we use the term inspiration to cover the concept of the whole process by which the Word comes to us. Initially it comes from the mouth of God (speaking, of course, metaphorically). From its origin in God it is then transmitted through the agency of human writers under divine supervision and superintendence. The next step in the process of communication is the apprehension of the divine message by human beings. It is explicitly stated in this article that the precise mode by which God accomplishes inspiration remains a mystery. The document makes no attempt to define the "how" of divine inspiration or even to suggest that the method is known to us.

The word inspiration can be used and has been used in our language to refer to moments of genius-level insight, of intensified states of consciousness or of heightened acts of human achievement. We speak of inspired poetry, meaning that the author achieved levels of insight and brilliance that are extraordinary. However, in this dimension of "inspiration" no suggestion is at hand that the source of inspiration is divine power. There are human levels of inspiration reflected in heroic acts, brilliant insights, and intensified states of consciousness. But that is not what is meant by the theological use of the term inspiration. Here the statement is making clear that by divine inspiration something transcending all human states of inspiration is in view, something in which the power and supervision of God are at work. Thus, the articles are saying that the Bible, though it is a human book insofar as it is written by human writers, has its humanity transcended by virtue of its divine origin and inspiration.

ARTICLE VIII
Human Authors

We affirm that God in His work of inspiration utilized the distinctive personalities and literary styles of the writers whom He had chosen and prepared.

We deny that God, in causing these writers to use the very words that He chose, overrode their personalities.

Article VIII reiterates that God's work of inspiration does not cancel out the humanity of the human writers he uses to accomplish his purpose. The writers of Scripture were chosen and prepared by God for their sacred task. However, whatever the process of inspiration may have been, it does not include the canceling of the personality of the writers as they wrote. Though the word is not used in the article, what is clearly in view is a denial of any kind of mechanistic or mechanical inspiration. Mechanical inspiration would reduce the human authors to the level of automatons, robot-like machines. An analysis of Scripture makes clear that the distinctive personalities and writing styles vary from one human writer to another. The style, for example, of St. Luke is obviously different from that of Matthew. The literary structures found in the writing of Daniel differ greatly from those found, for example, in the writing of James. Men of Hebrew origin tended to write in Hebraic styles, and those of the Greek cultural background tended to write in a Greek style. However, through divine inspiration God made it possible for his truth to be communicated in an inspired way making use of the backgrounds, personalities and literary styles of these various writers. The human writers were not machines and ought not to be conceived of as being without personality. What is overcome or overridden by inspiration is not human personality, style or literary structure, but human tendencies to distortion, falsehood and error.

The Word of God and Inerrancy

Articles IX through XII deal with the matter of greatest present concern: inerrancy. They seek to define terms and answer the chief questions that have been raised: If the Bible has come to us through human authors, which the earlier articles acknowledge, and if it is natural for human beings to err, which all confess, isn't the Bible necessarily errant? Doesn't it cease to be authentically human if it does not have errors? Again, if inerrancy applies properly only to the original manuscript, called autographs, and if we do not possess these, as we do not, isn't the argument for inerrancy meaningless? Or doesn't it stand only by appealing to documents that do not exist and whose inerrant state cannot be verified? Why can't inerrancy be applied to those parts of the Bible that deal with salvation and not to those parts that deal with history, science and other "unimportant" and "non-essential" matters?

ARTICLE IX
Inerrancy

> **We affirm** that inspiration, though not conferring omniscience, guaranteed true and trustworthy utterance on all matters of which the biblical authors were moved to speak and write.
>
> **We deny** that the finitude or fallenness of these writers, by necessity or otherwise, introduced distortion or falsehood into God's Word.

The affirmation of Article IX indicates that inspiration guarantees that the writings of Scripture are true and trustworthy. That is, they are not false, deceptive, or fraudulent in what they communicate.

As we dealt with the problem of the limitations of human language in Article IV, so we face now the difficulty of the speaking of truth by creatures who are not omniscient. It is one thing for God to confer infallibility to the writings and quite another to confer omniscience to the writers. Omniscience and infallibility must be carefully distinguished. Although in God they are cojoined, for man it is different. Omniscience refers to the scope of one's knowledge and infallibility, not to the reliability of his pronouncements. One who knows better can make a false statement if his intentions are to deceive. And, vice versa, a person with limited knowledge can make infallible statements if they can be guaranteed to be completely reliable. Thus we say that though the biblical writings are inspired, this does not imply thereby that the writers knew everything there was to be known or that they were infallible of themselves. The knowledge that they communicate is not comprehensive, but it is true and trustworthy as far as it goes.

The denial of Article IX has to do with man's propensity as a finite and fallen creature to introduce distortion or falsehood into God's Word. This was covered from another angle in Article IV. But what is in view here is the recurring charge that verbal inspiration or a confession of the inerrancy of Scripture carries with it a docetic view of Scripture. Docetism applies to a particular distortion of the biblical view of Jesus. In the earliest days of the Christian church there were those, usually associated with the school of gnosticism, who believed that Jesus did not really have a human nature or a human body. They argued that he only seemed or appeared to have a human body. This heresy was called docetism from the Greek word *dokeo* which means to seem, to think or to appear. Those who denied the reality of the incarnation and maintained that Jesus had but a phantom body were accused of this heresy. In a more refined and sophisticated sense docetism has come to apply to any failure to take seriously the real limitations of the human nature of Jesus.

The charge of biblical docetism has been leveled against advocates of inerrancy, most notably by Karl Barth. He accuses us of holding a view of inspiration in which the true humanity of the biblical writers is canceled out by the intrusion of the divine characteristics of infallibility. For Barth it is fundamental to our humanity that we are liable to error. If the classic statement is *errare est humanum*, to err is human, we reply that though it is true that a common characteristic of mankind is to err, it does not follow that men always err or that error is necessary for humanity. If such were to be the case, then it would be necessary for us to assert that Adam, before he fell, had to err or that he was not human. And we must also assert that in heaven, in a state of glorification and perfected sanctification, we must continue to err if we are to continue to be human. Not only must we ascribe such error to Adam before the fall and to glorified Christians, we would also have to apply it to the incarnate Christ. Error would be intrinsic to his humanity, and it would have been necessary for Jesus to distort the truth in order to be fully human. Let us never engage in such blasphemy even though we confess the depth to which we have fallen and the high degree of the propensity that we do have to err. Even apart from inspiration, it is not necessary for a human being to err in order to be human. So if it is possible for an uninspired person to speak the truth without error, how much more will it be the case for one who is under the influence of inspiration?

Finitude implies a necessary limitation of knowledge but not necessarily a distortion of knowledge. The trustworthy character of the biblical text should not be denied on the ground of man's finitude.

ARTICLE X
The Autographs

We affirm that inspiration, strictly speaking, applies only to the autographic text of Scripture, which in the providence of God can be ascertained from available manuscripts with great accuracy.

We further affirm that copies and translations of Scripture are the Word of God to the extent that they faithfully represent the original.

We deny that any essential element of the Christian faith is affected by the absence of the autographs.

> **We further deny** that this absence renders the assertion of biblical inerrancy invalid or irrelevant.

Article X deals directly with the perennial issue of the relationship of the text of Scripture that we presently have to the original documents which have not been preserved except through the means of copies. In the first instance, inspiration applies strictly to the original autographs of Scripture, to the original works of the inspired authors. What this does indicate is that the infallible control of God in the production of the original Scripture has not been miraculously perpetuated through the ages in the copying and translating process. It is plainly apparent that there are some minute variations between the manuscript copies that we possess and that the translating process will inject additional variants for those who read the Scripture in a language other than Hebrew or Greek. So the framers of the document are not arguing for a perpetually inspired transmission of the text.

Since we do not have the original manuscripts, some have urged that an appeal to the lost originals renders the whole case for the inspiration of the Scripture irrelevant. To reason in this manner is to denigrate the very serious work that has been done in the field of textual criticism. Textual criticism is the science which seeks to reconstruct an original text by a careful analysis and evaluation of the manuscripts we presently possess. This task has to be accomplished with respect to all documents from antiquity that have reached us through manuscript copies. The Old and New Testament Scriptures are probably the texts which have reached us with the most extensive and reliable attestation. For more than ninety-nine percent of the cases the original text can be reconstructed to a practical certainty. Even in the few cases where some perplexity remains, this does not impinge on the meaning of Scripture to the point of clouding a tenet of the faith or a mandate of life. Thus, in the Bible as we have it (and as it is conveyed to us through faithful translations) we do have for practical purposes the very word of God, inasmuch as the manuscripts do convey to us the complete vital truth of the originals.

The further affirmation of Article X is that copies and translations of Scripture are the Word of God to the extent that they faithfully represent the original. Though we do not actually possess the originals, we have such well reconstructed translations and copies that to the extent to which they do correspond to the original documents they may be said to be the Word of God. But because of the evident presence of copy errors and errors of translation the distinction must be made between the original work of inspiration in the autographs and the human labor of translating and copying those autographs.

The denial has in view the important point that in those minuscule segments of existing manuscripts where textual criticism has not been able to ascertain with absolute certainty what the original reading was, no essential article of the Christian faith is affected.

To limit inerrancy or inspiration to the original manuscripts does not make the whole contention irrelevant. It does make a difference. If the original text were errant, the church would have the option of rejecting the teachings of that errant text. If the original text is inerrant (and the science of textual criticism must be depended upon to reconstruct that inerrant text), we have no legitimate basis for disobeying a mandate of Scripture where the text is not in doubt. For example, if two theologians agreed that the original text were inerrant and if both agreed as to what the present copy taught and further agreed that the present copy was an accurate representation of the original, then it would follow irresistibly that the two men would be under divine obligation to obey that text. If, on the other hand, we asserted that the original manuscripts were possibly errant and the two theologians then agreed as to what the Bible taught and also agreed that the present translation or copy faithfully represented the original, neither would be under moral obligation to submit to the teachings of that possibly errant original. Therein lies the important issue of the relevancy of the character of the original manuscript.

ARTICLE XI
Infallibility

We affirm that Scripture, having been given by divine inspiration, is infallible, so that, far from misleading us, it is true and reliable in all the matters it addresses.

We deny that it is possible for the Bible to be at the same time infallible and errant in its assertions. Infallibility and inerrancy may be distinguished, but not separated.

The central affirmation of Article XI is the infallibility of Scripture. Infallibility is defined in this context in positive terms as implying the truthfulness and reliability of all matters that Scripture addresses. Negatively, infallibility is defined as the quality of that which does not mislead.

The denial of Article XI touches a very important point of controversy, particularly in the modern era. There are those who maintain that the Bible is infallible but not inerrant. Thus, infallibility is separated from inerrancy. The denial argues that it is not possible to maintain with consistency that something is at the same time infallible and errant in its assertions. To maintain such a disjunction between infallibility and inerrancy would involve a glaring contradiction.

Though the words infallible and inerrant have often been used interchangeably and virtually as synonyms in our language, nevertheless there remains a historic, technical distinction between the two words. Infallibility has to do with the question of ability or potential. That which is infallible is said to be unable to make mistakes or to err. The distinction here between that definition of infallible and the definition of inerrant is the distinction between the potential and the actual, the hypothetical and the real. That which is inerrant is that which in fact does not err. Again, theoretically, something may be fallible and at the same time inerrant. That is, it would be possible for someone to err who in fact does not err. However, the reverse is not true. If someone is infallible, that means he cannot err and if he cannot err, then he does not err. To assert that something is infallible yet at the same time errant is either to distort the meaning of "infallible" and/or "errant," or else to be in a state of confusion. Thus, infallibility and inerrancy in this sense cannot be separated though they may indeed be distinguished in terms of meaning. But anything that is infallible, that is, is incapable of erring, cannot at the same time err. For if it errs, it proves that it is capable of erring and therefore is not infallible.

In situations where infallibility has been substituted for inerrancy it has usually been designed to articulate a lower view of Scripture than that indicated by the word inerrant. In fact, however, the term infallibility in its original and technical meaning is a higher term than the term inerrant. Again, it is important to see that something which is fallible could theoretically be inerrant. But that which is infallible could not theoretically be at the same time errant.

ARTICLE XII
Inerrancy of the Whole

We affirm that Scripture in its entirety is inerrant, being free from all falsehood, fraud or deceit.

We deny that biblical infallibility and inerrancy are limited to spiritual, religious or redemptive themes, exclusive of assertions in the fields of history and science.

We further deny that scientific hypotheses about earth history may properly be used to overturn the teaching of Scripture on creation and the flood.

Article XII affirms clearly and unambiguously the inerrancy of sacred Scripture. In the affirmation the meaning of inerrancy is given in negative terms: that which is inerrant is "free from falsehood, fraud or deceit." Here inerrancy is defined by the way of negation, by establishing parameters beyond which we may not move, boundaries we may not transgress. An inerrant Scripture cannot contain falsehood, fraud or deceit in its teachings or assertions.

The denial explicitly rejects the tendency of some to limit infallibility and inerrancy to specific segments of the biblical message, such as spiritual, religious or redemptive themes, excluding assertions from the fields of history or science. It has been fashionable in certain quarters to maintain that the Bible is not normal history, but is redemptive history with the accent on redemption. Theories are then established that would limit inspiration to the redemptive theme of redemptive history allowing the historical dimension of redemptive history to be errant. However, the fact that the Bible is not written like other forms of history does not negate the historical dimension with which it is intimately involved. Though the Bible is indeed *redemptive* history, it is also redemptive *history*, and this means that the acts of salvation wrought by God actually occurred in the space-time world.

With respect to matters of science, the further denial that scientific hypotheses about earth history may be used to overturn the teaching of Scripture on such matters as creation and the flood again rejects the idea that the Bible speaks merely in areas of spiritual value or concerning redemptive themes. The Bible does have something to say about the origin of the earth, about the advent of man, about creation, and about such matters that have scientific import, such as the question of the flood. It is important to note that the second denial, "that scientific hypotheses about earth history may not be used to overturn the teaching of Scripture on matters such as the creation and the flood," does not carry with it the implication that scientific hypotheses or scientific research are useless to the student of the Bible or that science never has anything to contribute to an understanding of biblical material. It merely denies that the actual teaching of Scripture can be overturned by teachings from external sources.

To illustrate the intention of the second denial of Article XII, recall the classic example of the church's debate with the scientific community in the Middle Ages over the question of geocentricity and heliocentricity. The church had adopted the ancient Ptolemaic view that the earth was the center of the universe. Hence, the concept of geocentricity. Scientific inquiry and studies, particularly attending the advent of the telescope, led many scholars to believe that the sun, not the earth, was the center at least of our solar system, for the evidence from the scientific community for the centrality of the sun rather than the earth was seen to be compelling and overwhelming. We remember with embarrassment that Galileo was condemned as a heretic for asserting heliocentricity against what the church believed to be the teaching of Scripture. However, the scientific discoveries made it necessary for the church to re-examine the teaching on Scripture to see whether or not Scripture actually taught geocentricity or if this was an inference read into the Scripture on the basis of an earlier world view. Upon re-examining what Scripture really taught, the church came to the conclusion that there was no real conflict with science on this question of geocentricity because the Bible did not in fact in any place explicitly teach or assert that the earth was the center of either the solar system or the universe. Here the advances of science helped the church to correct an earlier misinterpretation of Scripture. To say that science cannot overturn the teaching of Scripture is not to say that science cannot aid the church in understanding Scripture, or even correct false inferences drawn from Scripture or actual misinterpretations of the Scripture. On the other hand, this does not give one license arbitrarily to reinterpret Scripture to force it into conformity to secular theories of origins or the like. For example, if the secular community asserts that the origin of humanity is the result of a cosmic accident or the product of blind, impersonal forces, such a view cannot possibly be reconciled with the biblical view of the purposive act of God's creation of mankind without doing radical violence to the Bible itself.

Questions of the extent of the flood or the literary genre of the earlier chapters of Genesis are not answered by this Statement. Questions of biblical interpretation that touch on the field of hermeneutics remain for further investigation and discussion. What the Scriptures actually teach about creation and the flood is not spelled out by this article; but it does spell out that whatever the Bible teaches about creation and the flood cannot be negated by secular theories.

The Word of God and Truth

The meaning of "truth" should be self-evident, but this has not been the case where discussions of the truthfulness of the Bible are concerned. What is truth? Some have argued that the Bible is not truthful unless it conforms to modern standards of scientific precision - no round numbers, precise grammar, scientific descriptions of natural phenomena, and so forth. Others have taken an entirely opposite view, arguing that the Bible is truthful so long as it attains its general spiritual ends, regardless of whether it actually makes false statements. Articles XIII through XV thread their way between these extremes. They maintain that the Bible is to be evaluated by its own principles of truth, which do not necessarily include modern forms of scientific expression, but argue at the same time that the statements of Scripture are always without error and, therefore, do not mislead the reader in any way. Article XIV deals with the way apparent discrepancies involving problems not yet resolved should be handled.

ARTICLE XIII
Truth

We affirm the propriety of using inerrancy as a theological term with reference to the complete truthfulness of Scripture.

We deny that it is proper to evaluate Scripture according to standards of truth and error that are alien to its usage or purpose.

We further deny that inerrancy is negated by biblical phenomena such as a lack of modern technical precision, irregularities of grammar or spelling, observational descriptions of nature, the reporting of falsehoods, the use of hyperbole and round numbers, the topical arrangement of material, variant selections of material in parallel accounts, or the use of free citations.

With the combination of the affirmation and denial of Article XIII regarding the term inerrancy, it may seem to some that, in view of all the qualifications that are listed in the denial, this word is no longer a useful or appropriate term to use with respect to the Bible. Some have said that it has "suffered the death of a thousand qualifications." The same, of course, could be said about the word "God." Because of the complexity of our concept of God, it has become necessary to qualify in great detail the differences in what is being affirmed and what is being denied when we use the term God. Such qualifications do not negate the value of the word, but only serve to sharpen its precision and usefulness.

It is important to note that the word inerrancy is called a theological term by Article XIII. It is an appropriate theological term to refer to the complete truthfulness of Scripture. That is basically what is being asserted with the term inerrancy: that the Bible is completely true, that all its affirmations and denials correspond with reality. Theological terms other than inerrancy are frequently in need of qualification and cannot be taken in a crass, literal sense. For example, the term omnipotence, when used to refer to God, does not literally mean what it may seem to. That is, omnipotence does not mean that God can do anything. The omnipotence of God does not mean that God can lie or that God could die or that God could be God and not God at the same time and in the same relationship. Nevertheless, as a term that has reference to God's complete sovereign control and authority over the created world, omnipotence is a perfectly useful and appropriate term in our theological vocabulary.

Because the term inerrancy must be qualified, some have thought that it would be better to exclude it from the church's vocabulary. However, the qualifications of the term are not new nor are they particularly cumbersome, and the word serves as an appropriate safeguard from those who would attack the truthfulness of Scripture in subtle ways. When we speak of inerrancy, then, we are speaking of the fact that the Bible does not violate its own principles of truth. This does not mean that the Bible is free from grammatical irregularities or the like, but that it does not contain assertions which are in conflict with objective reality.

The first denial that "the Bible ought not to be evaluated according to standards of truth and error alien to its own use or purpose" indicates that it would be inappropriate to evaluate the Bible's internal consistency with its own truth claims by standards foreign to the Bible's own view of truth. When we say that the truthfulness of Scripture ought to be evaluated according to its own standards that means that for the Scripture to be true to its claim it must have an internal consistency compatible with the biblical concept of truth and that all the claims of the Bible must correspond with reality, whether that reality is historical, factual or spiritual.

The second denial gives us a list of qualifications that is not intended to be exhaustive but rather illustrative of the type of considerations which must be kept in mind when one seeks to define the word inerrancy.

Modern technical precision. Inerrancy is not vitiated by the fact, for example, that the Bible occasionally uses round numbers. To say that truth has been distorted when, for example, the size of a crowd or the size of an army is estimated in round numbers would be to impose a criterion of truth that is foreign to the literature under examination. When a newspaper even in modern times says that 50,000 people assembled for a football game they are not considered to be engaging in falsehood, fraud or deceit because they have rounded off a number of 49,878, for example, to 50,000. It is an appropriate use of quantitative measurement in historical reporting that does not involve falsehood.

Irregularities of grammar or spelling. Though it is more beautiful and attractive to speak the truth with a fluent style and proper grammar, grammatical correctness is not necessary for the expression of truth. For example, if a man were on trial for murder and was asked if he killed his wife on February 13, and replied "I ain't killed nobody never," the crudity of his grammar would have nothing to do with the truth or falsehood of his statement. He can hardly be convicted of murder because his plea of innocence was couched within the context of rough and "errant" grammar. Inerrancy is not related to the grammatical propriety or impropriety of the language of Scripture.

Observational descriptions of nature. With respect to natural phenomena it is clear that the Bible speaks from the perspective of the observer on many occasions. The Bible speaks of the sun rising and setting and of the sun moving across the heavens. From the perspective of common observation it is perfectly appropriate to describe things as they appear to the human eye. To accuse the Bible of denying planetary motion would again be to impose a foreign perspective and criterion on the Scriptures. No one is offended when the weatherman speaks of sunrises and sunsets. No one accuses the weather bureau of seeking to revert to a medieval perspective of geocentricity or of falsifying the weather forecast by speaking of sunsets and sunrises. Those terms are perfectly appropriate to describe things as they appear to the observer.

The reporting of falsehoods. Some have maintained that the Bible is not inerrant because it reports falsehoods such as the lies of Satan and the fraudulent teachings of false prophets. However, though the Bible does in fact contain false statements, they are reported as being lies and falsehoods. So this in no way vitiates the truth value of the biblical record, but only enhances it.

The use of hyperbole. The use of hyperbole has been appealed to as a technical reason for rejecting inerrancy. However, hyperbole is a perfectly legitimate literary device. Hyperbole involves the intentional exaggeration of a statement to make a point. It provides the weight of intensity and emphasis that would otherwise be lacking. That the Bible uses hyperbole is without doubt. That hyperbole vitiates inerrancy is denied. The framers of the document maintain that the use of hyperbole is perfectly consistent with the Bible's own view of truth.

Other matters, such as the topical arrangement of material, the use of free citations (for example, from the Old Testament by the New Testament writers) and various selections of material and parallel accounts, where different writers include some information that other writers do not have and delete some information that others include, in no way destroys the truthfulness of what is being reported. Though biblical writers may have arranged their material differently, they do not affirm that Jesus said on one occasion what he never said on that occasion. Neither are they claiming that another parallel account is wrong for not including what they themselves include. As an itinerant preacher Jesus no doubt said many similar things on different occasions.

By biblical standards of truth and error is meant the view used both in the Bible and in everyday life, viz., a correspondence view of truth. This part of the article is directed toward those who would redefine truth to relate merely to redemptive intent, the purely personal or the like, rather than to mean that which corresponds with reality. For example, when Jesus affirmed that Jonah was in "the belly of the great fish" this statement is true, not simply because of the redemptive significance the story of Jonah has, but also because it is literally and historically true. The same may be said of the New Testament assertions about Adam, Moses, David and other Old Testament persons as well as about Old Testament events.

ARTICLE XIV
Consistency

We affirm the unity and internal consistency of Scripture.

We deny that alleged errors and discrepancies that have not yet been resolved vitiate the truth claims of the Bible.

Because the Bible is the Word of God and reflects his truthful character, it is important to affirm that it is one. Though it contains much information of a wide diversity of scope and interest, nevertheless there is an internal unity and consistency to the Word of God that flows from the nature of God's truth. God's truthfulness brings unity out of diversity. God is not an author of incoherency or of contradiction. His Word is consistent as well as coherent.

The denial in Article XIV deals with the particular problems of harmonization between texts that appear to be contradictory and of a number of other alleged errors and discrepancies pointed out repeatedly by critics. It must be acknowledged that there are some as yet unresolved apparent discrepancies in Scripture. A great deal of careful scrutiny has been applied to the investigation of these, and that effort has yielded very positive results. A great many alleged contradictions have been resolved, some in the early church and others more recently. The trend has been in the direction of reducing problems rather than increasing them. New knowledge acquired about the ancient texts and the meaning of language in the biblical age as well as new discoveries coming from manuscripts and parchments uncovered by archaeology have given substantial help in resolving problems and have provided a solid basis for optimism with respect to future resolution of remaining difficulties. Difficulties that have not been resolved may yet be resolved under further scrutiny. This approach to the question of the resolution of difficulties may seem at first glance to be an exercise in "special pleading." However, if any work deserves special consideration it is sacred Scripture. Before we jump to the conclusion that we are faced with an ultimately unresolvable contradiction we must exhaust all possible illuminating research. A spirit of humility demands that we give careful attention to the resolutions that have already been made, and that we acknowledge that we have not as yet left every stone unturned in our efforts to give a fair and judicious hearing to the text of the Bible. Some of the greatest discoveries that have helped us to understand the Bible have come about because we have been forced to dig more deeply in our efforts to reconcile difficulties within the text. It should not be deemed strange that a volume that included sixty-six different books written over 1,400 hundred years would have some difficulties of harmonization within it.

It has often been charged that the Bible is full of contradictions. Such statements are unwarranted by the evidence. The amount of seriously difficult passages compared to the total quantity of material found there is very small indeed. It would be injudicious and even foolhardy for us to ignore the truth claims of the Bible simply because of presently unresolved difficulties. We have a parallel here with the presence of anomalies in the scientific world. Anomalies may indeed be so significant that they make it necessary for scientists to rethink their theories about the nature of geology, biology or the like. For the most part, however, when an overwhelming weight of evidence points to the viability of a theory and some anomalies remain that do not seem to fit the theory, it is not the accepted practice in the scientific world to "scrap" the whole well-attested theory because of a few difficulties that have not yet been resolved. With this analogy in science we may be bold to say that when we approach

Scripture as we do, we do nothing more or less than apply the scientific method to our research of Scripture Itself.

Every student of Scripture must face squarely and with honesty the difficulties that are still unresolved. To do this demands our deepest intellectual endeavors. We should seek to learn from Scripture as we examine the text again and again. The unresolved difficulties, in the process of being resolved, often yield light to us as we gain a deeper understanding of the Word of God.

ARTICLE XV
Accommodation

We affirm that the doctrine of inerrancy is grounded in the teaching of the Bible about inspiration.

We deny that Jesus' teaching about Scripture may be dismissed by appeals to accommodation or to any natural limitation of His humanity.

In the affirmation of Article XV inerrancy as a doctrine is viewed as being inseparably related to the biblical teaching on inspiration. Though the Bible nowhere uses the word "inerrancy" the concept is found in the Scriptures. The Scriptures have their own claim to being the Word of God. The words of the prophets are prefaced by the statement, "Thus sayeth the Lord." Jesus speaks of the Scriptures of the Old Testament as being incapable of being broken (John 10:35). He says that not a jot or tittle of the law will pass away until all be fulfilled (Matt. 5:18). Paul tells us that all is given by inspiration (2 Tim. 3:16). Inerrancy is a corollary of inspiration inasmuch as it is unthinkable that God should inspire that which is fraudulent, false or deceitful. Thus, though the word "inerrancy" is not explicitly used in the Scriptures, the word "inspired" is, and the concept of inerrancy is designed to do justice to the concept of inspiration.

It should not be thought that because the Bible does not contain the terms "inerrant" or "inerrancy," there is therefore no biblical basis for the doctrine of inerrancy. The Bible nowhere uses the term "trinity," and yet the doctrine of the trinity is clearly taught throughout the New Testament. When the Church affirms a doctrine it finds no necessity to discover a verbal parallel between the doctrine and the words of the Bible itself. What is implied by the affirmation of this article is that the doctrine of the inerrancy of Scripture is a doctrine ultimately based upon the teaching of Jesus himself. The framers of this confession wish to express no higher nor lower view of Scripture than that held and taught by Jesus. That becomes explicit in the denial. The denial expresses that Jesus' teaching about Scripture may not be easily dismissed. It has been fashionable in recent Protestantism to grant that Jesus did indeed hold and teach a doctrine of inspiration that would comport with the concept of inerrancy but then to argue at the same time that Jesus' view is deficient in light of limitations tied to his human nature. The fact that Jesus held a view of inspiration such as he did is "excused" on the basis that, touching his human nature, Jesus was a product of his times. Jesus, it is urged, could not possibly have known all of the problems that have since been raised by higher criticism. As a result, Jesus like the rest of his contemporaries accepted uncritically the prevailing notion of Scripture of his own day. For example, when Jesus mentions that Moses wrote of him, he was unaware of the documentary hypothesis which would apparently demolish any serious case for Mosaic authorship of the first five books of the Old Testament.

From a Protestant perspective, such ignorance by Jesus concerning the truth about Scripture is excused on the basis that the only way he could have known the truth would be for him in his human nature to be omniscient. Now for Jesus in his human nature to be omniscient, that is to know all things, would involve a confusion of the divine and the human natures. Omniscience is an attribute of deity not of humanity. Since ordinarily Protestants do not believe that Jesus' human nature was deified with such attributes as omniscience, it appears perfectly understandable and excusable that in his lack of knowledge he made mistakes about the Scripture. This is the line of reasoning which the denial part of the article disallows.

The problems raised by these explanations are too numerous and too profound for a detailed treatment here. But the point is this. Even though we admit that Jesus in his human nature was not omniscient, we do urge that his claims to teach nothing by his own authority but by the authority of the Father (John 8:28) and to be the very incarnation of truth (John 14:6) would be fraudulent claims if anything that he taught were in error. Even if his error arose out of his ignorance, he would be guilty of sin for claiming to know truth that he in fact did not know. At stake here is our very redemption. For if Jesus taught falsely while claiming to be speaking the truth, he would be guilty of sin. If he were guilty of sin, then obviously his atonement could not atone for himself, let alone for his people. Ultimately the doctrine of Scripture is bound up with the doctrine of Jesus Christ. It is because of Jesus' high view of Scripture that the framers of this confession so strenuously maintain the high view of Scripture today.

Again, it is fashionable in many circles to believe Jesus when he speaks of heavenly matters, matters of redemption and salvation, but to correct Jesus when he speaks of historical matters such as the writing of the Pentateuch and other matters relating to the doctrine of Scripture. At this point those who accept Jesus when he speaks redemptively but reject him when he speaks historically violate a teaching principle that Jesus himself espoused. Jesus raised the rhetorical question, "How can you believe me concerning heavenly things when you cannot believe me concerning earthly things?" (John 3:12). It seems that we have a generation of scholars who are willing to believe Jesus concerning heavenly matters while rejecting those things which he taught about the earth. (What Jesus says concerning history may be falsified by critical methods, but what he says concerning heavenly matters is beyond the reach of verification or falsification.) The framers of this confession believe that Jesus' principle of the trustworthiness of his teaching as affecting both heavenly matters and earthly matters must be maintained even to this day.

The Word of God and You

Discussion of inerrancy is merely an academic exercise unless it concerns the individual Christian on the level of his growth in God. But this is precisely what it does. Confession of the full authority and inerrancy of Scripture should lead us to increasing conformity to the image of Christ, which is the God-ordained goal of every Christian. The final Articles of Affirmation and Denial deal with this matter, including the work of the Holy Spirit in helping the believer to understand and apply the Scriptures to his or her life.

ARTICLE XVI
Church History

We affirm that the doctrine of inerrancy has been integral to the Church's faith throughout its history.

We deny that inerrancy is a doctrine invented by Scholastic Protestantism, or is a reactionary position postulated in response to negative higher criticism.

This affirmation again speaks of the doctrine of inerrancy, not the word inerrancy. It is readily acknowledged that the word inerrancy was not used with any degree of frequency and perhaps not even at all before the seventeenth century. For example, Martin Luther nowhere uses the term inerrancy as a noun with respect to Scripture. Because of this some have said that Luther did not believe in inerrancy, but Luther argued that the Scriptures never "err." To say that the Scriptures never err is to say nothing more nor less than that the Bible is inerrant. So though the word inerrancy is of relatively modern invention, the concept is rooted not only in the biblical witness to Scripture itself but also in the acceptance of the vast majority of God's people throughout the history of the Christian church. We find the doctrine taught, embraced and espoused by men such as St. Augustine, Thomas Aquinas, Martin Luther, John Calvin, Jonathan Edwards, John Wesley, and a host of Christian scholars and teachers throughout the history of the church. While the language of inerrancy does not appear in Protestant confessions of faith until the modern ages, the concept of inerrancy is surely not foreign or strange to the confessions of east or west, Catholic or Protestant.

The denial follows the thinking of the affirmation closely. The denial is simply that inerrancy as a concept is not the product of a rigid, sterile, rationalistic approach to Scripture born of the scholastic movement of seventeenth century Protestantism. Nor is it proper to understand the doctrine as a twentieth century reaction to liberal theology or "modernism."

It is not the affirmation of inerrancy that is of recent vintage; it is its denial. It is not the reaction to higher criticism that is new, but its uncritically accepted philosophical assumptions of negative criticism that is a new phenomenon in mainline Christianity. Such criticism is not new in the sense that no one ever questioned the integrity or authenticity of Scripture in past ages, but the newness of the phenomenon is its widespread and easy acceptance within churches and by leaders who would claim allegiance to mainline Christianity.

ARTICLE XVII
Witness of the Spirit

We affirm that the Holy Spirit bears witness to the Scriptures, assuring believers of the truthfulness of God's written Word.

We deny that this witness of the Holy Spirit operates in isolation from or against Scripture.

Article XVII attests to the doctrine of the internal testimony of the Holy Spirit. That is to say, our personal conviction of the truth of Scripture rests not on the external evidences to the Scriptures truthfulness in and of themselves, but those evidences are confirmed in our hearts by the special work of God the Holy Spirit. The Spirit himself bears witness to our human spirit that the Scriptures are indeed the Word of God. Here God himself confirms the truthfulness of his own Word.

The denial guards against substituting a reliance upon the immediate guidance of the Holy Spirit for the content of Scripture itself. The thought behind the denial is that the Holy Spirit normally works in conjunction with the Scripture and speaks to us through the Scripture, not against the Scripture or apart from the Scripture. Word and Spirit are to be viewed together, Word bearing witness to the Spirit and being the means by which we test the spirits to see if they be of God (1 John 4:1) and the Spirit working within our hearts to confirm the Word of God to ourselves. Thus, there is reciprocity between Word and Spirit, and they are never to be set over against each other.

ARTICLE XVIII
Interpretation

We affirm that the text of Scripture is to be interpreted by grammatico-historical exegesis, taking account of its literary forms and devices, and that Scripture is to interpret Scripture.

We deny the legitimacy of any treatment of the text or quest for sources lying behind it that leads to relativizing, dehistoricizing, or discounting its teaching, or rejecting its claims to authorship.

Article XVIII touches on some of the most basic principles of biblical interpretation. Though this article does not spell out in detail a vast comprehensive system of hermeneutics, it nevertheless gives basic guidelines on which the framers of the confession were able to agree.

The first is that the text of Scripture is to be interpreted by grammatico-historical exegesis. Grammatico-historical is a technical term that refers to the process by which we take the structures and time periods of the written texts seriously as we interpret them. Biblical interpreters are not given the license to spiritualize or allegorize texts against the grammatical structure and form of the text itself. The Bible is not to be reinterpreted to be brought into conformity with contemporary philosophies but is to be understood in its intended meaning and word usage as it was written at the time it was composed. To hold to grammatico-historical exegesis is to disallow the turning of the Bible into a wax nose that can be shaped and reshaped according to modern conventions of thought. The Bible is to be interpreted as it was written, not reinterpreted as we would like it to have been written according to the prejudices of our own era.

The second principle of the affirmation is that we are to take account of the literary forms and devices that are found within the Scriptures themselves. This goes back to principles of interpretation espoused by Luther and the Reformers. A verb is to be interpreted as a verb; a noun as a noun, a parable as a parable, didactic literature as didactic literature, narrative history as narrative history, poetry as poetry, and the like. To turn narrative history into poetry, or poetry into narrative history would be to violate the intended meaning of the text. Thus, it is important for all biblical interpreters to be aware of the literary forms and grammatical structures that are found within the Scripture. An analysis of these forms is proper and appropriate for any correct interpretation of the text.

The third principle in the affirmation is that Scripture is to interpret Scripture. Historically, this principle is called the "analogy of faith." It rests on the previous affirmation that the Bible represents a unified, consistent and coherent Word from God. Any interpretation of a passage that yields a meaning in direct contradiction to another portion of Scripture is disallowed. It is when Scripture interprets Scripture that the sovereignty of the Holy Spirit, the supreme interpreter of the Bible, is duly acknowledged. Arbitrarily setting one part of Scripture against another would violate this principle. Scripture is to be interpreted therefore in terms not only of its immediate context but also of the whole context of the Word of God.

The denial part of Article XVIII decries the propriety of critical analyses of the text that produce a relativization of the Bible. This does not prohibit an appropriate quest for literary sources or even oral sources that may be discerned through source criticism but draws a line as to the extent to which such critical analysis can go. When the quest for sources produces a dehistoricizing of the Bible, a rejection of its teaching or a rejection of the Bible's own claims of authorship it has trespassed beyond its proper limits. This does not prohibit the external examination of evidence to discover the authorship of books that go unnamed in sacred Scriptures such as the epistle to the Hebrews. A search is even allowable for literary traditions that may have been brought together by a final editor whose name is mentioned in Scripture. It is never legitimate, however, to run counter to express biblical affirmations.

ARTICLE XIX
Health of the Church

We affirm that a confession of the full authority, infallibility and inerrancy of Scripture is vital to a sound understanding of the whole of the Christian faith. We further affirm that such confession should lead to increasing conformity to the image of Christ.

We deny that such confession is necessary for salvation. However, we further deny that inerrancy can be rejected without grave consequences, both to the individual and to the church.

Article XIX's affirmation speaks to the relevance of the doctrine of inerrancy to the life of the Christian. Here the functional character of biblical authority is in view. The article is affirming that the confession is not limited to doctrinal concern for theological purity but originates in a profound concern that the Bible remain the authority for the living out of the Christian life. It also recognizes that it is possible for people to believe in the inerrancy or infallibility of Scripture and lead godless lives. It recognizes that a confession of a doctrine of Scripture is not enough to bring us to sanctification but that it is a very important part of the growth process of the Christian that he should rest his confidence in the truthful revelation of the Word of God and thereby should be moved inwardly to conform to the image of Christ. A strong doctrine of the authority of Scripture should, when properly implemented, lead a person to a greater degree of conformity to that Word he espouses as true.

The denial in Article XIX is very important. The framers of the confession are saying unambiguously that confession of belief in the inerrancy of Scripture is not an essential of the Christian faith necessary for salvation. We gladly acknowledge that people who do not hold to this doctrine may be earnest and genuine, zealous and in many ways dedicated Christians. We do not regard acceptance of inerrancy to be a test for salvation. However, we urge as a committee and as an assembly that people consider the severe consequences that may befall the individual or church which casually and easily rejects inerrancy. We believe that history has demonstrated again and again that there is all too often a close relationship between rejection of inerrancy and subsequent defections from matters of the Christian faith that are essential to salvation. When the church loses its confidence in the authority of sacred Scripture the church inevitably looks to human opinion as its guiding light. When that happens, the purity of the church is direly threatened. Thus, we urge upon our Christian brothers and sisters of all professions and denominations to join with us in a reaffirmation of the full authority, integrity, infallibility and inerrancy of sacred Scripture to the end that our lives may be brought under the authority of God's Word, that we may glorify Christ in our lives, individually and corporately as the church.

BOOK V

EXPLAINING HERMENEUTICS

A COMMENTARY ON THE CHICAGO STATEMENT ON BIBLICAL HERMENEUTICS

Norman Leo Geisler

Copyright © 1983 Norman L. Geisler
All rights reserved.

COMMENTARY

NORMAN L. GEISLER

ARTICLE I
Authority of the Scriptures

We affirm that the normative authority of Holy Scripture is the authority of God Himself, and is attested by Jesus Christ, the Lord of the Church.

We deny the legitimacy of separating the authority of Christ from the authority of Scripture, or of opposing the one to the other.

This first article affirms that the authority of Scripture cannot be separated from the authority of God. Whatever the Bible affirms, God affirms. And what the Bible affirms (or denies), it affirms (or denies) with the very authority of God. Such authority is normative for all believers; it is the canon or rule of God.

This divine authority of Old Testament Scripture was confirmed by Christ Himself on numerous occasions (cf. Matt. 5:17-18; Luke 24:44; John 10:34-35). And what our Lord confirmed as to the divine authority of the Old Testament, He promised also for the New Testament (John 14:16; 16:13).

The Denial points out that one cannot reject the divine authority of Scripture without thereby impugning the authority of Christ, who attested Scripture's divine authority. Thus it is wrong to claim one can accept the full authority of Christ without acknowledging the complete authority of Scripture.

ARTICLE II
The Written Word and the Incarnated Word

We affirm that as Christ is God and Man in one Person, so Scripture is, indivisibly, God's Word in human language.

We deny that the humble, human form of Scripture entails errancy any more than the humanity of Christ, even in His humiliation, entails sin.

Here an analogy is drawn between Christ and Scripture. Both Christ and Scripture have dual aspects of divinity and humanity, indivisibly united in one expression. Both Christ and Scripture were conceived by an act of the Holy Spirit. Both involve the use of fallible human agents. But both produced a theanthropic result; one a sinless person and the other an errorless book. However, like all analogies, there is a difference. Christ is one person uniting two natures whereas Scripture is one written expression uniting two authors (God and man). This difference notwithstanding, the strength of the likeness in the analogy points to the inseparable unity between divine and human dimensions of Scripture so that one aspect cannot be in error while the other is not.

The Denial is directed at a contemporary tendency to separate the human aspects of Scripture from the divine and allow for error in the former. By contrast the framers of this article believe that the human form of Scripture can no more be found in error than Christ could be found in sin. That is to say, the Word of God (i.e., the Bible) is as necessarily perfect in its human manifestation as was the Son of God in His human form.

ARTICLE III
The Centrality of Jesus Christ

We affirm that the person and work of Jesus Christ are the central focus of the entire Bible.

We deny that any method of interpretation which rejects or obscures the Christ-centeredness of Scripture is correct.

This Affirmation follows the teaching of Christ that He is the central theme of Scripture (Matt. 5:17; Luke 24:27, 44; John 5:39; Heb. 10:7). This is to say that focus on the person and work of Christ runs throughout the Bible from Genesis to Revelation. To be sure there are other and tangential topics, but the person and work of Jesus Christ are central.

In view of the focus of Scripture on Christ, the Denial stresses a hermeneutical obligation to make this Christocentric message clear in the expounding of Scripture. As other articles (cf. Article XV) emphasize the "literal" interpretation of Scripture, this article is no license for allegorization and unwarranted typology which see Christ portrayed in every detail of Old Testament proclamation. The article simply points to the centrality of Christ's mission in the unfolding of God's revelation to man.

Neither is there any thought in this article of making the role of Christ more ultimate than that of the Father. What is in view here is the focus of Scripture and not the ultimate source or object of the whole plan of redemption.

ARTICLE IV
The Role of the Holy Spirit in Revelation

We affirm that the Holy Spirit who inspired Scripture acts through it today to work faith in its message.

We deny that the Holy Spirit ever teaches to any one anything which is contrary to the teaching of Scripture.

Here stress is laid on the fact that the Holy Spirit not only is the source of Scripture, but also works to produce faith in Scripture He has inspired. Without this ministry of the Holy Spirit, belief in the truth of Scripture would not occur.

The Denial is directed at those alleged "revelations" which some claim to have but which are contrary to Scripture. No matter how sincere or genuinely felt, no dream, vision, or supposed revelation which contradicts Scripture ever comes from the Holy Spirit. For the utterances of the Holy Spirit are all harmonious and noncontradictory (see Article XX).

ARTICLE V
The Role of the Holy Spirit in Application

We affirm that the Holy Spirit enables believers to appropriate and apply Scripture to their lives.

We deny that the natural man is able to discern spiritually the biblical message apart from the Holy Spirit.

The design of this article is to indicate that the ministry of the Holy Spirit extends beyond the inspiration of Scripture to its very application to the lives of the believer. Just as no one calls Jesus Lord except by the Holy Spirit (I Cor. 12:3), so no one can appropriate the message of Scripture to his life apart from the gracious work of the Holy Spirit.

The Denial stresses the truth that the natural man does not receive the spiritual message of Scripture. Apart from the work of the Holy Spirit there is no welcome for its truth in an unregenerate heart.

This does not imply that a non-Christian is unable to understand the meaning of any Scripture. It means that whatever he may perceive of the message of Scripture, that without the Holy Spirit's work he will not welcome the message in his heart.

ARTICLE VI
Propositional Truth Corresponds to Reality

We affirm that the Bible expresses God's truth in propositional statements, and we declare that biblical truth is both objective and absolute. We further affirm that a statement is true if it represents matters as they actually are, but is an error if it misrepresents the facts.

We deny that, while Scripture is able to make us wise unto salvation, biblical truth should be defined in terms of this function. We further deny that error should be defined as that which willfully deceives.

Since hermeneutics is concerned with understanding the truth of Scripture, attention is directed here to the nature of truth. Several significant affirmations are made about the nature of truth.

First, in contrast to contemporary relativism it is declared that truth is absolute. Second, as opposed to subjectivism it is acknowledged that truth is objective. Finally, in opposition to existential and pragmatic views of truth, this article affirms that truth is what corresponds to reality. This same point was made in the "Chicago Statement on Inerrancy" (1978) in Article XIII and the commentary on it.

The Denial makes it evident that views which redefine an error to mean what "misleads," rather than what is a mistake, must be rejected. This redefinition of the word "error" is both contrary to Scripture and to common sense. In Scripture the word error is used of unintentional acts (Lev. 4:2) as well as intentional ones. Also, in common parlance a statement is in error if it is a factual mistake, even if there was no intention to mislead anyone by it. So to suggest that the Bible contains mistakes, but that these are not errors so long as they do not mislead, is contrary to both Scripture and ordinary usage.

By this subtle redefinition of error to mean only what misleads but not what misrepresents, some have tried to maintain that the Bible is wholly true (in that it never misleads) and yet that it may have some mistakes in it. This position is emphatically rejected by the confessors of this document.

ARTICLE VII
One Meaning, Multiple Applications

We affirm that the meaning expressed in each biblical text is single, definite, and fixed.

We deny that the recognition of this single meaning eliminates the variety of its application.

The Affirmation here is directed at those who claim a "double" or "deeper" meaning to Scripture than that expressed by the authors. It stresses the unity and fixity of meaning as opposed to those who find multiple and pliable meanings. What a passage means is fixed by the author and is not subject to change by readers. This does not imply that further revelation on the subject cannot help one come to a fuller understanding, but simply that the meaning given in a text is not changed because additional truth is revealed subsequently.

Meaning is also definite in that there are defined limits by virtue of the author's expressed meaning in the given linguistic form and cultural context. Meaning is determined by an author; it is discovered by the readers.

The Denial adds the clarification that simply because Scripture has one meaning does not imply that its messages cannot be applied to a variety of individuals or situations. While the interpretation is one, the applications can be many.

ARTICLE VIII
Cultural Universality

We affirm that the Bible contains teachings and mandates which apply to all cultural and situational contexts and other mandates which the Bible itself shows apply only to particular situations.

We deny that the distinction between the universal and particular mandates of Scripture can be determined by cultural and situational factors. We further deny that universal mandates may ever be treated as culturally or situationally relative.

In view of the tendency of many to relativize the message of the Bible by accommodating it to changing cultural situations, this Affirmation proclaims the universality of biblical teachings. There are commands which transcend all cultural barriers and are binding on all men everywhere. To be sure, some biblical injunctions are directed to specific situations, but even these are normative to the particular situation(s) to which they speak. However, there are commands in Scripture which speak universally to the human situation and are not bound to particular cultures or situations.

The Denial addresses the basis of the distinction between universal and particular situations. It denies that the grounds of this distinction are relative or purely cultural. It further denies the legitimacy of relativizing biblical absolutes by reducing them to purely cultural mandates.

The meaning of this article is that whatever the biblical text means is binding. And what is meant to be universally binding should not be relegated to particular situations any more than what is meant to apply only to particular circumstances should be promulgated as universally applicable.

There is an attempt here to strike a balance between command and culture by recognizing that a command transcends culture, even though it speaks to and is expressed in a particular culture. Thus while the situation (or circumstances) may help us to discover the right course of action, the situation never determines what is right. God's laws are not situationally determined.

ARTICLE IX
Hermeneutics and Meaning

> *We affirm* that the term hermeneutics, which historically signified the rules of exegesis, may properly be extended to cover all that is involved in the process of perceiving what the biblical revelation means and how it bears on our lives.
>
> *We deny* that the message of Scripture derives from, or is dictated by, the interpreter's understanding. Thus we deny that the "horizons" of the biblical writer and the interpreter may rightly "fuse" in such a way that what the text communicates to the interpreter is not ultimately controlled by the expressed meaning of the Scripture.

The primary thrust of this Affirmation is definitional. It desires to clarify the meaning of the term hermeneutics by indicating that it includes not only perception of the declared meaning of a text but also an understanding of the implications that text has for one's life. Thus, hermeneutics is more than biblical exegesis. It is not only the science that leads forth the meaning of a passage but also that which enables one (by the Holy Spirit) to understand the spiritual implications the truth(s) of this passage has for Christian living.

The Denial notes that the meaning of a passage is not derived from or dictated by the interpreter. Rather, meaning comes from the author who wrote it. Thus the reader's understanding has no hermeneutically definitive role. Readers must listen to the meaning of a text and not attempt to legislate it. Of course, the meaning listened to should be applied to the reader's life. But the need or desire for specific application should not color the interpretation of a passage.

ARTICLE X
Adequacy of Variety of Literary Forms

We affirm that Scripture communicates God's truth to us verbally through a wide variety of literary forms.

We deny that any of the limits of human language render Scripture inadequate to convey God's message.

This Affirmation is a logical literary extension of Article II which acknowledges the humanity of Scripture. The Bible is God's Word, but it is written in human words; thus, revelation is "verbal." Revelation is "propositional" (Article II) because it expresses certain propositional truth. Some prefer to call it "sentential" because the truth is expressed in sentences. Whatever the term—verbal, propositional, or sentential—the Bible is a human book which uses normal literary forms. These include parables, satire, irony, hyperbole, metaphor, simile, poetry, and even allegory (e.g., Ezek. 16-17).

As an expression in finite, human language, the Bible has certain limitations in a similar way that Christ as a man had certain limitations. This means that God adapted Himself through human language so that His eternal truth could be understood by man in a temporal world.

Despite the obvious fact of the limitations of any finite linguistic expression, the Denial is quick to point out that these limits do not render Scripture an inadequate means of communicating God's truth. For while there is a divine adaptation (via language) to human finitude there is no accommodation to human error. Error is not essential to human nature. Christ was human and yet He did not err. Adam was human before he erred. So simply because the Bible is written in human language does not mean it must err. In fact, when God uses human language there is a supernatural guarantee that it will not be in error.

ARTICLE XI
Adequacy of Translation

We affirm that translations of the text of Scripture can communicate knowledge of God across all temporal and cultural boundaries.

We deny that the meaning of biblical texts is so tied to the culture out of which they came that understanding of the same meaning in other cultures is impossible.

Simply because the truth of Scripture was conveyed by God in the original writings does not mean that it cannot be translated into another language. This article affirms the translatability of God's truth into other cultures. It affirms that since truth is transcendent (see Article XX) it is not culture-bound. Hence the truth of God expressed in a first-century culture is not limited to that culture. For the nature of truth is not limited to any particular medium through which it is expressed.

The Denial notes that since meaning is not inextricably tied to a given culture it can be adequately expressed in another culture. Thus the message of Scripture need not be relativized by translation. What is expressed can be the same even though how it is expressed differs.

ARTICLE XII: Limits for Functional Equivalence Translation

We affirm that in the task of translating the Bible and teaching it in the context of each culture, only those functional equivalents that are faithful to the content of biblical teaching should be employed.

We deny the legitimacy of methods which either are insensitive to the demands of cross-cultural communication or distort biblical meaning in the process.

Whereas the previous article treated the matter of the translatability of divine truth, this article speaks to the adequacy of translations. Obviously not every expression in another language will appropriately convey the meaning of Scripture. In view of this, caution is urged that the translators remain faithful to the truth of the Scripture being translated by the proper choice of the words used to translate it.

This article treats the matter of "functional" equivalence. Often there is no actual or literal equivalence between expressions in one language and a word-for-word translation into another language. What is expressed (meaning) is the same but how it is expressed (the words) is different. Hence a different construction can be used to convey the same meaning.

The Denial urges sensitivity to cultural matters so that the same truth may be conveyed, even though different terms are being used. Without this awareness missionary activity can be severely hampered.

ARTICLE XIII
The Value and Limits of Genre Criticism

We affirm that awareness of the literary categories, formal and stylistic, of the various parts of Scripture is essential for proper exegesis, and hence we value genre criticism as one of the many disciplines of biblical study.

We deny that generic categories which negate historicity may rightly be imposed on biblical narratives which present themselves as factual.

The awareness of what kind of literature one is interpreting is essential to a correct understanding of the text. A correct genre judgment should be made to ensure correct understanding. A parable, for example, should not be treated like a chronicle, nor should poetry be interpreted as though it were a straightforward narrative. Each passage has its own genre, and the interpreter should be cognizant of the specific kind of literature it is as he attempts to interpret it. Without genre recognition an interpreter can be misled in his understanding of the passage. For example, when the prophet speaks of "trees clapping their hands" (Isa. 55:12) one could assume a kind of animism unless he recognized that this is poetry and not prose.

The Denial is directed at an illegitimate use of genre criticism by some who deny the truth of passages which are presented as factual. Some, for instance, take Adam to be a myth, whereas in Scripture he is presented as a real person. Others take Jonah to be an allegory when he is presented as a historical person and so referred to by Christ (Man. 12:40-42). This Denial is an appropriate and timely warning not to use genre criticism as a cloak for rejecting the truth of Scripture.

ARTICLE XIV
Literary Forms and Factual History

We affirm that the biblical record of events, discourses and sayings, though presented in a variety of appropriate literary forms, corresponds to historical fact.

We deny that any such event, discourse or saying reported in Scripture was invented by the biblical writers or by the traditions they incorporated.

This article combines the emphases of Articles VI and XIII. While acknowledging the legitimacy of literary forms, this article insists that any record of events presented in Scripture must correspond to historical fact. That is, no reported event, discourse, or saying should be considered imaginary.

The Denial is even clearer than the Affirmation. It stresses that any discourse, saying, or event reported in Scripture must actually have occurred. This means that any hermeneutic or form of biblical criticism which claims that something was invented by the author must be rejected. This does not mean that a parable must be understood to represent historical facts, since a parable does not (by its very genre) purport to report an event or saying but simply to illustrate a point.

ARTICLE XV
The Grammatical-Historical Sense

We affirm the necessity of interpreting the Bible according to its literal, or normal, sense. The literal sense is the grammatical-historical sense, that is, the meaning which the writer expressed. Interpretation according to the literal sense will take account of all figures of speech and literary forms found in the text.

We deny the legitimacy of any approach to Scripture that attributes to it meaning which the literal sense does not support.

The literal sense of Scripture is strongly affirmed here. To be sure the English word literal carries some problematic connotations with it. Hence the words normal and grammatical-historical are used to explain what is meant. The literal sense is also designated by the more descriptive title grammatical-historical sense. This means the correct interpretation is the one which discovers the meaning of the text in its grammatical forms and in the historical, cultural context in which the text is expressed.

The Denial warns against attributing to Scripture any meaning not based in a literal understanding, such as mythological or allegorical interpretations. This should not be understood as eliminating typology or designated allegory or other literary forms which include figures of speech (see Articles X, XIII, and XIV).

ARTICLE XVI
Roles and Varieties of Biblical Criticism

We affirm that legitimate critical techniques should be used in determining the canonical text and its meaning.

We deny the legitimacy of allowing any method of biblical criticism to question the truth or integrity of the writer's expressed meaning, or of any other scriptural teaching.

Implied here is an approval of legitimate techniques of "lower criticism" or "textual criticism." It is proper to use critical techniques in order to discover the true text of Scripture, that is, the one which represents the original one given by the biblical authors.

Whereas critical methodology can be used to establish which of the texts are copies of the inspired original, it is illegitimate to use critical methods to call into question whether something in the original text is true. In other words, proper "lower criticism" is valid but negative "higher criticism" which rejects truths of Scripture is invalid.

ARTICLE XVII
Scripture is Self-Interpreting

We affirm the unity, harmony, and consistency of Scripture and declare that it is its own best interpreter.

We deny that Scripture may be interpreted in such a way as to suggest that one passage corrects or militates against another. We deny that later writers of Scripture misinterpreted earlier passages of Scripture when quoting from or referring to them.

Two points are made in the Affirmation, the unity of Scripture and its self-interpreting ability. Since the former is treated elsewhere (Article XXI), we will comment on the latter here. Not only is the Bible always correct in interpreting itself (see Article XVIII), but it is the "best interpreter" of itself.

Another point made here is that comparing Scripture with Scripture is an excellent help to an interpreter. For one passage sheds light on another. Hence the first commentary the interpreter should consult on a passage is what the rest of Scripture may say on that text.

The Denial warns against the assumption that an understanding of one passage can lead the interpreter to reject the teaching of another passage. One passage may help him better comprehend another but it will never contradict another.

This last part of the Denial is particularly directed to those who believe the New Testament writers misinterpret the Old Testament, or that they attribute meaning to an Old Testament text not expressed by the author of that text. While it is acknowledged that there is sometimes a wide range of application for a text, this article affirms that the interpretation of a biblical text by another biblical writer is always within the confines of the meaning of the first text.

ARTICLE XVIII
Meaning may Transcend Human Understanding

We affirm that the Bible's own interpretation of itself is always correct, never deviating from, but rather elucidating, the single meaning of the inspired text. The single meaning of a prophet's words includes, but is not restricted to, the understanding of those words by the prophet and necessarily involves the intention of God evidenced in the fulfillment of those words.

We deny that the writers of Scripture always understood the full implications of their own words.

This Affirmation was perhaps the most difficult to word. The first part of the Affirmation builds on Article VII which declared that Scripture has only one meaning, and simply adds that whenever the Bible comments on another passage of Scripture it does so correctly. That is, the Bible never misinterprets itself. It always correctly understands the meaning of the passage it comments on (see Article XVII). For example, that Paul misinterprets Moses is to say that Paul erred. This view is emphatically rejected in favor of the inerrancy of all Scripture.

The problem in the second statement of the Affirmation revolves around whether God intended more by a passage of Scripture than the human author did. Put in this way, evangelical scholars are divided on the issue, even though there is unity on the question of "single meaning." Some believe that this single meaning may be fuller than the purview of the human author, since God had far more in view than did the prophet when he wrote it. The wording here is an attempt to include reference to the fulfillment of a prophecy (of which God was obviously aware when He inspired it) as part of the single meaning which God and the prophet shared. However, the prophet may not have been conscious of the full implications of this meaning when he wrote it.

The way around the difficulty was to note that there is only one meaning to a passage which both God and the prophet affirmed, but that this meaning may not always be fully "evidenced" until the prophecy is fulfilled. Furthermore, God, and not necessarily the prophets, was fully aware of the fuller implications that would be manifested in the fulfillment of this single meaning.

It is important to preserve single meaning without denying that God had more in mind than the prophet did. A distinction needs to be made, then, between what God was conscious of concerning an affirmation (which, in view of His foreknowledge and omniscience, was far more) and what He and the prophet actually expressed in the passage. The Denial makes this point clear by noting that biblical authors were not always fully aware of the implications of their own affirmations.

ARTICLE XIX
Danger in Preunderstandings

We affirm that any preunderstandings which the interpreter brings to Scripture should be in harmony with scriptural teaching and subject to correction by it.

We deny that Scripture should be required to fit alien preunderstandings, inconsistent with itself, such as naturalism, evolutionism, scientism, secular humanism, and relativism.

The question of preunderstanding is a crucial one in contemporary hermeneutics. The careful wording of the Affirmation does not discuss the issue of whether one should approach Scripture with a particular preunderstanding, but simply which kinds of preunderstanding one has are legitimate. This question is answered by affirming that only those preunderstandings which are compatible with the teaching of Scripture are legitimate. In fact, the statement goes further and demands that all preunderstanding be subject to "correction" by the teaching of Scripture.

The point of this article is to avoid interpreting Scripture through an alien grid or filter which obscures or negates its true message. For it acknowledges that one's preunderstanding will affect his understanding of a text. Hence to avoid misinterpreting Scripture one must be careful to examine his own presuppositions in the light of Scripture.

ARTICLE XX
Extrabiblical Sources

We affirm that since God is the author of all truth, all truths, biblical and extrabiblical, are consistent and cohere, and that the Bible speaks truth when it touches on matters pertaining to nature, history, or anything else. We further affirm that in some cases extrabiblical data have value for clarifying what Scripture teaches, and for prompting correction of faulty interpretations.

We deny that extrabiblical views ever disprove the teaching of Scripture or hold priority over it.

What is in view here is not so much the nature of truth (which is treated in Article VI), but the consistency and coherence of truth.

This is directed at those views which consider truth paradoxical or contradictory. This article declares that a proper hermeneutic avoids contradictions, since God never affirms as true two propositions, one of which is logically the opposite of the other.

Further, this Affirmation recognizes that not all truth is in the Bible (though all that is affirmed in the Bible is true). God has revealed Himself in nature and history as well as in Scripture. However, since God is the ultimate Author of all truth, there can be no contradiction between truths of Scripture and the true teachings of science and history.

Although only the Bible is the nonnative and infallible rule for doctrine and practice, nevertheless what one learns from sources outside Scripture can occasion a reexamination and reinterpretation of Scripture. For example, some have taught the world to be square because the Bible refers to "the four corners of the earth" (Isa. 11:12). But scientific knowledge of the spherical nature of the globe leads to a correction of this faulty interpretation. Other clarifications of our understanding of the biblical text are possible through the study of the social sciences.

However, whatever prompting and clarifying of Scripture that extrabiblical studies may provide, the final authority for what the Bible teaches rests in the text of Scripture itself and not in anything outside it (except in God Himself). The Denial makes clear this priority of the teaching of God's scriptural revelation over anything outside it.

ARTICLE XXI
Harmony of General and Special Revelations

We affirm the harmony of special with general revelation and therefore of biblical teaching with the facts of nature.

We deny that any genuine scientific facts are inconsistent with the true meaning of any passage of Scripture.

This article continues the discussion of the previous article by noting the harmony of God's general revelation (outside Scripture) and His special revelation in Scripture. It is acknowledged by all that certain interpretations of Scripture and some opinions of scientists will contradict each other. However, it is insisted here that the truth of Scripture and the facts of science never contradict each other.

"Genuine" science will always be in accord with Scripture. Science, however, based on naturalistic presuppositions will inevitably come in conflict with the supernatural truths of Scripture. Far from denying a healthy interchange between scientific theory and biblical interpretation, the framers of this statement welcome such. Indeed, it is acknowledged (in article XX) that the exegete can learn from the scientist. What is denied is that we should accept scientific views that contradict Scripture or that they should be given an authority above Scripture.

ARTICLE XXII
Genesis 1-11 as Factual

We affirm that Genesis 1-11 is factual, as is the rest of the book.

We deny that the teachings of Genesis 1-11 are mythical and that scientific hypotheses about earth history or the origin of humanity may be invoked to overthrow what Scripture teaches about creation.

Since the historicity and the scientific accuracy of the early chapters of the Bible have come under severe attack it is important to apply the "literal" hermeneutic espoused (Article XV) to this question. The result was a recognition of the factual nature of the account of the creation of the universe, all living things, the special creation of man, the Fall, and the Flood. These accounts are all factual, that is, they are about space-time events which actually happened as re-ported in the book of Genesis (see Article XIV).

The article left open the question of the age of the earth on which there is no unanimity among evangelicals and which was beyond the purview of this conference. There was, however, complete agreement on denying that Genesis is mythological or unhistorical. Likewise, the use of the term "creation" was meant to exclude the belief in macro-evolution, whether of the atheistic or theistic varieties.

ARTICLE XXIII
Perspicacity of the Scriptures

We affirm the clarity of Scripture and specifically of its message about salvation from sin.

We deny that all passages of Scripture are equally clear or have equal bearing on the message of redemption.

Traditionally this teaching is called the "perspicuity" of Scripture. By this is meant that the central message of Scripture is clear, especially what the Bible says about salvation from sin.

The Denial disassociates this claim from the belief that everything in Scripture is clear or that all teachings are equally clear or equally relevant to the Bible's central saving message. It is obvious to any honest interpreter that the meaning of some passages of Scripture is obscure. It is equally evident that the truth of some passages is not directly relevant to the overall plan of salvation.

ARTICLE XXIV
The Value of Biblical Scholarship

We affirm that a person is not dependent for understanding of Scripture on the expertise of biblical scholars.

We deny that a person should ignore the fruits of the technical study of Scripture by biblical scholars.

This article attempts to avoid two extremes. First, it affirms that one is not dependent on biblical "experts" for his understanding of the basic truths of Scripture. Were this not true, then a significant aspect of the priesthood of all believers would be destroyed. For if the understanding of the laity is contingent on the teaching of experts, then Protestant interpretive experts will have replaced the teaching magisterium of Catholic priests with a kind of teaching magisterium of Protestant scholars.

On the other hand, biblical scholars do play a significant role in the lay understanding of Scripture. Even the very tools (Bible, dictionaries, concordances, etc.) used by laypersons to interpret Scripture were produced by scholars. And when it comes to more technical and precise understanding of specific Scripture the work of experts is more than helpful. Hence the implied exhortation in the denial to avail oneself of the fruit of scholarship is well taken.

ARTICLE XXV
Preaching as Exposition of Scriptural Texts

We affirm that the only type of preaching which sufficiently conveys the divine revelation and its proper application to life is that which faithfully expounds the text of Scripture as the Word of God.

We deny that the preacher has any message from God apart from the text of Scripture.

This final article declares that good preaching should be based in good hermeneutics. The exposition of Scripture is not to be treated in isolation from the proclamation of Scripture. In preaching the preacher should faithfully expound the Word of God. Anything short of a correct exposition of God's written Word is pronounced insufficient.

Indeed, the Denial declares that there is no message from God apart from Scripture. This was understood not to contradict the fact that there is a general revelation (affirmed in Article XXI) but simply to note that the only inspired and infallible writing from which the preacher can and must preach is the Bible.

Evangelicals at a Fork in the Road
by Jay Grimstead, 1977

Today Christian leaders and theologians in large numbers are burdened for the health of the church. Their concern is specific. They see the evangelical church absorbing an alarming amount of false teaching about Scripture through some of its theological leadership and they note its consequences. Their concern is for evangelicals: those people who have trusted Christ for their salvation and in whom the Holy Spirit lives, but who are unwittingly erring.

Numbers of evangelical theologians have accepted many negative theories of historical criticism of the bible which in years past were held by those who went by the name of "liberal." Some have also accepted an "existential" view of truth and how to know truth, often through the influence of Karl Barth, and are slipping into a theology which used to go by the name of "neo-orthodoxy." Several, like G. C. Berkouwer, (who seems to be the theological rallying point for this new view of Scripture over the past 20 or 30 years. They now embrace a more liberal view and are in the process of quietly trying to <u>redefine evangelicalism after their own image</u>. Thus, even words such as "infallible," which used to carry unmistakable meaning, are being so redefined that one no longer knows what is meant by a statement of faith which claims "infallibility."

Some evangelical theologians who claim to hold to "infallibility" are teaching essentially the same view of Scripture that the theological liberal, Charles Augustus Briggs held in 1980. Briggs claimed that the Bible was true only where it spoke of matters of faith, but not necessarily where it spoke of matters of history and nature. From 1890 to 1940, this view was called the "liberal" view by evangelicals. And now it is proclaimed by some as the "evangelical view" and as the very view which was held by the church for 2,000 years. Because of his view of Scripture, Briggs was condemned for heresy by the Presbyterian General Assembly in 1893 and suspended from the ministry.

In recent months a new evangelical organization called The International Council on Biblical Inerrancy has been formed to face this problem. Its purpose is "to take a united stand over a period of ten years to elucidate, vindicate, and apply in the fields of academic theology and practical Christian instruction, the doctrine of Biblical inerrancy as an essential element for the authority of Scripture and the health of the church, and to attempt to win back that portion of the church which has drifted away from this position."

James Boice, pastor of Tenth Presbyterian Church in Philadelphia is chairman of the 50-member board. Serving with Boice on the Executive Council are Gleason Archer, Edmund Clowney, Norman Geisler, John Gerstner, Jay Grimstead, Harold Hoehner, Dan Hoke, Miss A. Wetherell Johnson, Kenneth Kantzer, J.I. Packer, J. Barton Payne, Robert Prues, Earl Radmacher, Francis Schaeffer and R.C. Sproul.

Many evangelicals who are alerted to the declining view of Scripture find themselves emotionally resistant to having the issues clarified or to having any brother referred to as wrong. The response of many is, "Let's just love each other, and preach the Gospel and not worry about these theological differences." Unknown to them is the high correlation between evangelicals holding to this new, liberalized view of Scripture and their departing from orthodoxy in other areas of Christian doctrine and lifestyle, such as:

1. A denial of a literal Adam and Eve
2. Universalism
3. A loose and open view on premarital or homosexual sex
4. Rejection of Christ's "hard line" on divorce or Paul's view of marriage in Ephesians 5 as normative
5. A tendency to look at the Bible through the eyes of modern psychology rather than *visa versa*

If the historical view of verbal inerrancy is rejected outright or is merely tolerated as one of several optional views of Scripture, there is no logical necessity as such laid upon the church why it should continue to believe in the deity of Christ or the substitutionary atonement.

If the evangelical church at all levels does not awake to this departure from the historical view of Scripture (held by Christ, the Apostles, the Medieval Church, the Reformers, Wesley, Edwards, Spurgeon, Strong, Hodge, Warfield and down to evangelicals of our own century), it will become incapable of standing for or recognizing God's truth. In this relativistic age Biblical living will increasingly become more difficult and more costly.

Plans for the International Council on Biblical Inerrancy for the next ten years involve two major thrusts: academic defense of the inerrancy position and practical Christian instruction. The academic theology will lay the foundation of scholarly work needed for the church to proceed on the basis of a Bible that is true in whatever it touches. The four major areas where work will be done are Biblical studies, historical studies, theological and philosophical studies, and practical theology. The project will take the coordinated effort of an army of scholars.

The second major thrust of the Council is to offer theological training for pastors, Christian workers, and laypersons regarding inerrancy and related to local coalitions of those pastors, laypersons, and Christian workers, who are committed to an inerrant Bible and who are eager to join hands across lines of denominational and theological distinctive.

A short-term educational package dealing specifically with inerrancy is being developed for use in local churches and colleges. Other forms of more sophisticated theological education for pastors and laypersons are being explored. A national network of conferences and traveling seminars is being planned on a five-year basis beginning January 1979. Speakers for these will be drawn from the ranks of the ICBI coalition.

To launch the ICBI, the Council has planned a summit meeting for some 300 evangelical leaders and theologians in Chicago, October 26-29, 1978. During the preceding year, twelve papers will be written, edited and circulated which will form the theological bases on which a statement on Scripture will be written. These white papers will be read by the summit conferees prior to the conference and will be thoroughly discussed at the conference. A statement of Scripture will evolve based on the discussion of these papers. It is hoped that conferees will leave the summit with a plan in their hands for influencing their world.

White papers will deal with a definition of inerrancy and supposed "errors"; Biblical autographs; the adequacy of human language to communicate final, absolute truth; the non-docetic view of truly human authors writing inerrant sentences; the inner witness of the Holy Spirit; the view of Scriptures held by Christ and the Apostles; the view held by the Reformers; higher criticism; legitimate hermeneutics; the effect of the presuppositions of Kant, Kierkegaard, and Barth on the present discussion; and the Lordship of Christ and Biblical authority.

Soon after the Summit meeting, a three-year schedule of dialogues is planned to carry on technical conversation with those scholars who are opposed to inerrancy. These will be forums where clarification and understanding can take place. These dialogues will serve two functions. First, they will clarify many sub-issues related to inerrancy and eliminate some misunderstandings and some straw men from the controversy. Second, they will provide an opportunity for scholars who differ on these issues to meet and show the church and the world how to disagree in love. Friendships established at such meetings can begin softening and mellowing any journalistic debates.

Some will charge those who hold to inerrancy with making mountains out of mole hills and with dividing the evangelical church. On the contrary, they are simply calling a "mountain" a "mountain," and think it is reasonable to expect that the ICBI will be a great, transdenominational, unifying force within evangelicalism, as it encourages Christian brothers and sisters across the nation to join hands in standing for the only objective foundation there is for revealed information from God ... His inerrant Scripture.

Thousands of pastors, scholars, and informed laypersons see the decline of Biblical inerrancy as the foundational problem for most other doctrinal and lifestyle problems facing the church today. They are therefore, eater to be a part of any movement which will stand tall for God's propositional truth and carry out its program in a thoughtful, scholarly, and loving way. Old, backward theological feuds over such issues as dispensationalism, baptism, church government, Calvinism-Arminianism, evangelism technique, apologetic approaches, and many other denominational and theological distinctives will be transcended in this pan-evangelical, unified front standing together on God's inerrant, written Word.

Though a firm and clear stand on God's propositional truth will be taken by each ICBI member, the Council trusts the Church will not see it repeating the same harshness which was characteristic of some who defended this same position in the 1920's and 1930's. The Council assumes that evangelicals committed to inerrancy will continue to work hand in hand will all other evangelicals for such common causes as world evangelization and hunger relief, and against such common foes as Bultmanian liberalism, the occult, and abortion on demand. The ICBI thus hopes to foster "a coalition within a coalition," and sees the inner coalition of inerrancy evangelicals as the "hard core" which keeps providing strength for evangelicalism as a whole and, without which, evangelicalism would eventually crumple and fall under the increasing strains coming upon it from secular culture.

The ICBI prayerfully urges all evangelicals who feel this same burden to write to our office and let us know if they would be interested in participating in some way with this movement's national and local ten-year, educational thrust. We particularly need to be in touch at a local level with pastors, teachers, writers, and with laymen who have time to invest in such a cause. All who send in their name will be placed on our mailing list and will receive progress reports and articles written by ICBI members.

The educational tasks before us in both writing and instruction is not a "brain washing" effort. We do not desire to tell just one side of the story. Our goal is to so educate pastors and laypersons of the choices before them regarding Biblical authority that they will <u>base their choice on facts and clear thinking</u> rather than just choose their view of Scripture because a given choice takes less effort, or because someone they respect has chosen that view.

Jay Grimstead, Jim Boice

Patterson, Gerstner, Geisler

Tony Evans and Michael E. Haynes

Made in United States
North Haven, CT
17 October 2025